Teaching as Protest

Teaching as Protest explores how K-12 teachers can expand the boundaries of their profession with anti-oppressive, community-building pedagogies. Now more than ever, students are looking to their schools to make meaning of our nation's complicated and compounded traumas, namely those at the intersection of race, class, gender, and power. This book provides historical and philosophical perspectives into liberatory instructional work, while offering planning, preparation, and practice tools whose modalities recognize identities and mindsets, emphasizing schools that predominantly serve Black students. By moving beyond conventional tools and tasks such as standards, lesson-planning, and grade-team meetings and into more emancipatory, student-centered approaches, teachers can answer the call to a more just and radical demonstration of protest intended to disrupt and dismantle oppression, racism, and bias.

Dr. Robert S. Harvey is Superintendent of East Harlem Scholars Academies, a community-based network of PK-12 schools, and Chief Academic Officer of East Harlem Tutorial Program, where he manages Out-of-School Time, Postsecondary, and Teaching Residency programs. A Visiting Professor in the Practice of Public Leadership at Memphis Theological Seminary, Dr. Harvey is an education leader, community connector, author, and public voice in education, child advocacy, and social change with extensive experience in academic and non-profit leadership.

Susan Gonzowitz is the founding Managing Director of the East Harlem Teaching Residency, a 28-month, school-based teacher development program of East Harlem Tutorial Program. An Adjunct Lecturer in Literacy and Racial Equity at Hunter College School of Education (CUNY), Ms. Gonzowitz is a teacher developer, consultant, and author committed to pedagogy, antiracism, and literacy.

Also by Robert S. Harvey, from
Eye on Education

Abolitionist Leadership in Schools:
Undoing Systemic Injustice Through
Communally Conscious Education

Teaching as Protest

Emancipating Classrooms Through Racial Consciousness

Robert S. Harvey with Susan Gonzowitz

NEW YORK AND LONDON

Cover Image: Shutterstock

First published 2022
by Routledge
605 Third Avenue, New York, NY 10158

and by Routledge
4 Park Square, Milton Park, Abingdon, Oxon, OX14 4RN

Routledge is an imprint of the Taylor & Francis Group, an informa business

© 2022 Robert S. Harvey and Susan Gonzowitz

The right of Robert S. Harvey and Susan Gonzowitz to be identified as authors of this work has been asserted in accordance with sections 77 and 78 of the Copyright, Designs and Patents Act 1988.

All rights reserved. No part of this book may be reprinted or reproduced or utilised in any form or by any electronic, mechanical, or other means, now known or hereafter invented, including photocopying and recording, or in any information storage or retrieval system, without permission in writing from the publishers.

Trademark notice: Product or corporate names may be trademarks or registered trademarks, and are used only for identification and explanation without intent to infringe.

Library of Congress Cataloging-in-Publication Data
Names: Harvey, Robert S. (Educator), author.
Title: Teaching as protest: emancipating classrooms through racial consciousness / Robert S. Harvey with Susan Gonzowitz.
Description: New York, NY: Routledge, 2022. | Includes bibliographical references.
Identifiers: LCCN 2021044567 (print) | LCCN 2021044568 (ebook) | ISBN 9781032020464 (hardback) | ISBN 9781032024394 (paperback) | ISBN 9781003183365 (ebook)
Subjects: LCSH: African Americans—Education—
Social aspects. | Student-centered learning—United States. | Social justice—United States. | Racism—United States.
Classification: LCC LC2717 .H38 2022 (print) | LCC LC2717 (ebook) | DDC 371.829/96073—dc23/eng/20211006
LC record available at https://lccn.loc.gov/2021044567
LC ebook record available at https://lccn.loc.gov/2021044568

ISBN: 9781032020464 (hbk)
ISBN: 9781032024394 (pbk)
ISBN: 9781003183365 (ebk)

DOI: 10.4324/9781003183365

Typeset in Palatino
by codeMantra

Contents

Acknowledgements vii
About the Authors ix

1 The Moral Arc of Pedagogical Protest: From Resistance to Reimagination 1
   Robert S. Harvey

2 Disordered Attachments: The Risks and Revolution of Identities Work 29
   Robert S. Harvey

3 An Appeal to White Folx in White Spaces: What Are We Giving Up? 57
   Susan Gonzowitz

4 But If Faced With Courage: Talk About History in Today's Context 75

5 Two Sides of the Same Coin: Talk About Power, Not Only Oppression 95

6 Just Another Day: Talk About the Everydayness of Race 113

7 How Does It Feel to *Not* Be a Problem? Talk About Whiteness 127

8 Ain't I A Human? Talk About Personhood, Not Production 143

9 And Ways to Grow: Talk About a
   Literacy as a Tool 159

10 The World Can't Take It Away: Talk About Joy 171

   Conclusion: On Inconvenience 185

Acknowledgements

To the memories of my ancestors—the earliest teachers of protest, personhood, and democratic possibility. What I know, today, as an ethic of protest is what my ancestral pedagogues knew as an inescapable burden of responsibility to what *could be*.

To the imaginations of the young people who continuously shape who I am and how I navigate the world—to the ones who ground the source of my being as an educator and invite me to make meaning of the world with them. Their hopes and enthusiasm, frankness and criticism, and insights and radicalism are the ecosystem that incubated the intellectual pursuits of this text. After spending a seminar with students navigating the nexus of protests, national memory, moral argument, and race, I am thankful for the many ways our students trust us to guide them into and through the world around them. Without them, we mislay our meaning.

A deep amount of gratitude goes to those who made space as deep listeners, allowing me to wrestle with ideas and philosophies, thinkers, and practitioners without imposing boundaries to the fluidity of the wrestling. I have come to honor the impact of deep listening as a praxis of being and doing community, and I cherish those who were exemplars of being and doing community during the writing of this book.

In the end, I owe each of you deep gratitude. Gratitude for your willingness to trust my witness in pursuing an emancipated hope for teaching and learning in this world.

—Dr. Robert S. Harvey

The journey towards becoming an abolitionist educator is never ending. Every class of teacher candidates and aspiring school leaders I have worked with has challenged me and forced me to think more carefully about the work. The stories they have shared, the vulnerabilities they have shown, and the pedagogical risks they have been willing to take have made this book possible.

Alongside them, a phenomenal group of education leaders have taught me to think differently and more expansively about this work. Without my mentors, colleagues, and friends, I would not be the practitioner I am today.

Thank you, Dawan Julien, for starting me out on my journey toward becoming a more social justice-oriented educator. You opened my eyes and changed the trajectory of all of the teacher preparation work I do.

Thank you, Dr. Sherryl Brown Graves. I could not ask for a better mentor. Your partnership, stories, humor, pushes, and patience have made wading through even the most bureaucratic moments tolerable. I appreciate how much I have learned about life, teaching, and motherhood from you.

Thank you, Veronika Herrera Mojica, for working with me to reimagine teacher preparation and pedagogy. You have been an amazing colleague, sounding board, and friend. I am a better educator because we are on the same team.

Thank you, Linara Davidson Greenidge, for grounding me and always being the voice of reason through your difficult questions, for your thoughtful challenges to my perspectives, and for your constant encouragement to give grace.

Thank you, most of all, to my amazing husband, Porfirio Gonzowitz. I could not have worked on this book or become the educator I am without you. With your passion, drive, and love you have shown me every day what it means to center the humanity of young people. You have been willing to test my theories, challenge my thinking, and find meaning in my messiest writing. Thank you for being my constant thought partner, editor, and inspiration.

—Susan Gonzowitz

About the Authors

 **Dr. Robert S. Harvey** is an educator and writer, faith leader, community connector, child advocate, and public scholar. Drawing on lived experiences, ethical thought, and a bold vision for the future of human wellbeing, his leadership and writing has a threefold focus—love, justice, and hope—with young people at the heart.

He is the Superintendent of East Harlem Scholars Academies, a community-based network of public charter schools (PreK-12th) in New York City, and Chief Academic Officer of East Harlem Tutorial Program, managing a multisite out-of-school time and postsecondary access and success program, public engagement, and a teaching residency. He is also a Visiting Professor in the Practice of Public Leadership at Memphis Theological Seminary.

Prior to his work in New York City, he was Head of School at Star Academy College Preparatory, a public charter school in Memphis, Tennessee. Before Memphis, he was Chief Operating Officer and Senior Lecturer in Religion and the Social Sciences at Simmons College of Kentucky, an historically Black college in Louisville, Kentucky. Dr. Harvey started his academic career working in Independent day and boarding schools, as teaching faculty, director of extended day, dean of students, and as director of admissions and financial aid. Throughout his work, he has led with and embodied a deep commitment to antiracism, radical humanity, and faith-informed justice.

Dr. Harvey has committed himself to lifelong learning through a doctorate in leadership and society from Memphis Theological Seminary, master of theological studies from Harvard University, and bachelor of arts from Bryant University. He also earned a certificate of school management and leadership (CSML) from Harvard Graduate School of Education, and has completed the Harvard Institute for Superintendents and District Leaders.

He is author of *Abolitionist Leadership in Schools: Undoing Systemic Injustice through Communally Conscious Education* (Routledge), which works from an abolitionist lineage to guide education and community-based leaders in providing preemptive, premeditated, and progressive leadership while countering the impacts of racism that endure in our schools and communities. His opinions on education and justice have been published by Education Post, Education Week, Chalkbeat, Education Dive, TheGrio, Blavity, St. Louis Post-Dispatch, and a variety of academic journals. Beyond academia and writing, he serves on a variety of nonprofit boards impacting education, community and economic investment, and the arts.

Susan Gonzowitz is an educator, teacher developer, consultant, and author committed to pedagogy, antiracism, and literacy.

She is the founding Managing Director of the East Harlem Teaching Residency (EHTR), a 28-month, school-based teacher development program within East Harlem Tutorial Program (EHTP). She designed the residency to focus on developing teachers, namely, teachers of color, committed to teaching in East Harlem (New York City). She is also an adjunct lecturer in literacy and racial equity at Hunter College School of Education (CUNY).

Before designing and launching the residency, Susan worked for three years as the Director of Out-of-School (OST) Elementary Program at EHTP and has been instrumental in thought-partnering and leading EHTP's racial-equity work. Prior to EHTP, she worked within the New York City Department of Education as an instructional coach and elementary school teacher.

Susan co-authored a chapter, "High Leverage Resident Practices," for *The Teacher Residency Model: Core Components for High Impact on Student Achievement*, and has written several articles on race, literacy, and teaching. She has also presented on her work at the American Association of College for Teachers, American Educational Research Association, National Center for Teaching Residencies, and New York Association of Colleges for Teacher Education, TeachingWorks, and a host of other workshops and conferences.

She is currently a doctor of education (EdD) student in educational leadership, administration, and policy at Fordham University, received her master's degree in literacy and an advanced certification in school supervision and administration at Hunter College, and her undergraduate degree in elementary education and teaching from Skidmore College. She is also licensed in New York State 1–6 elementary education, birth-6 literacy education, and school building and school district leadership.

1

The Moral Arc of Pedagogical Protest: From Resistance to Reimagination

Robert S. Harvey

"I'm not your friend. I'm not your homegirl. I'm not your daddy. I'm *sure* not your momma, and I'm not even one of your little favorite teachers," she uttered, flat-footed with a resolute stare in her eyes, as we rushed to a quiet only rivaled by the hollowed emptiness of a cathedral. We stared ahead—"not a creature was stirring, not even a mouse"—as we awaited what she'd say to color her opening remark with context. She moved toward the pedestal podium, symmetrically centered to the chalkboard, and she leaned in our direction.

As we basked in the mystery of her antics, an innocently intrigued classroom of Black and white and Indian sixth graders, she faintly smirked, knowing that she had our undivided attention. She continued, "I have one responsibility—to teach. And you have one responsibility—to make meaning of what I teach." Seeing our faces, not only mesmerized but also contorted by the failed expectation of not hearing the usual refrain of our supposed responsibility, "to learn," she replied as only she could.

DOI: 10.4324/9781003183365-1

Fix your faces, because you heard me, and you heard me right. Your only responsibility in *this* class, and I can't speak for the rest of 'em, is to make meaning of what you learn. You don't have to accept any of it as truth if you don't want to, and if I do this the right way, you ought to question some of it—especially the stuff I *have* to teach you. Because questioning what you learn is part of what it means to make meaning of what you learn. And not only questioning it, but doubting it, and critiquing it—all of which are forms of *protest*. And why do I want you to become students who know how to protest what you learn? Because in this sixth-grade social studies class, we are going to talk about the history of the United States, but all history, the way you read it and the way you hear it, a'int the truth.

To what would have ordinarily been a rambunctious group of 11- and 12-year-olds, Mrs. Inez Tayborn became the embodiment of an American tradition—the protest tradition. The radically contrarian approach she espoused—that "all history, the way you read it and the way you hear it, ain't the truth"—was the moral act of protest and pedagogy that, as preteens, we needed but didn't realize it. It might be that she was a child of the forties and fifties. It might be that she was the child, and grandchild, of sharecroppers. It might be that she was a migrant from small-town Mississippi, "a state sweltering with the heat of injustice, sweltering with the heat of oppression,"[1] to St. Louis, Missouri. It might be that she recalled with clarity the venomous cry, "Segregation Now! Segregation Forever!" being broadcasted across the country from the lips of Governor George Wallace. It might be that she had dedicated more than five decades—*50-plus years*—of her life to educating predominantly Black and brown young people with the memories of her own lived truths and traumas in this nation. It might be that the politics of the so-called "Negro problem" were more than history taught, but history experienced. Whatever it was, she believed in the moral arc of protest—and she knew that while it *could* bend, it would *not* bend unaided. The classroom was her lever of resistance and her canvas of creation.

We would often enter into her curtain-drawn classroom, met by the words from the 1971 classic, "What's Going On," bellowed with the gospel-inspired rasp of Marvin Gaye. And if not Gaye, it was the pernicious, high-pitched funk falsetto of James Brown and the young folx from Watts and Compton in Los Angeles in 1968, exclaiming, "Say it loud, I'm black and I'm proud."

Mrs. Tayborn never articulated it this way, but music—the sounds of the Black lived experience in this nation—readied the physical space in which we engaged in pedagogical protest. In many ways, it was her embodied understanding that "the language of poetry and art lifts and elevates the human spirit by touching the emotive chords of wonder, hope, and mystery."[2] The rhythm and the lyrics were, movingly, a clarion call to our youthful conscience. It invited us to wonder what and how we might question, doubt, or critique the knowledge we'd absorb, without ignoring our responsibility to make meaning of it for ourselves, for our communities, and for the world around us. And while numerous teachers elected silence, she risked polarization, castigation, and termination to guide us in shaping our protest imagination. Those three characteristics—*questioning*, *doubting*, and *critiquing*—are conceptually, in effect, the catalyzing stimuli for protesting the status quo, abolishing oppression, and imagining the future. We had all three.

Since its beginning, this country has affirmed an apotheosized declaration of ideals—"that all men are created equal, that they are endowed by their Creator with certain unalienable Rights, that among these are Life, Liberty and the pursuit of Happiness"—against the anti-Black backdrop of chattel slavery, penal labor, and eventually mass incarceration. Protests and protest rhetoric, throughout this history, have responded to the myriad ways in which the powerful have exploited the gap between American idealization and American reality. From the German Coast Uprising in 1811, when enslaved folx marched from sugar plantations to New Orleans, to Nat Turner's Slave Rebellion in 1831, to the March on Washington for Jobs and Freedom in 1963, to Bloody Sunday in 1965 on the Edmund Pettus Bridge (Selma), to the 2020 demonstrations all across the globe affirming that Black Lives Matter, protests on the basis of racial justice have been catalyzed by a sole aim: holding [white] America accountable for its whiteness. Protests in all of its forms—boycotts, rebellions, assemblies, marches, strikes, sit-ins, petitions, and riots—by and for Black folx have historically *never* been coupled with or guided by an allegiance to American whiteness and its progenies: white supremacy, capitalism, militarism, statism, authoritarianism, imperialism, ableism, and every other ism and phobia born of whiteness. Not whiteness as a skin color, but whiteness as a sociopolitical and socioeconomic arrangement built on the premise of white superiority that operates beneath the consciousness in every facet of American public life. In fact, protests as an ethic have always been about struggling *against* the progenies of whiteness, imagining just alternatives, and calling for the ruling classes, typically conspirators within and perpetuators of whiteness, to yield power as a means of realizing this nation's declaration of ideals. As such, protests and protest rhetoric repudiate the idea that the realization of a human-centered and justice-leaning ideals are bestowed by the powerful; rather, they are the result of struggle and sacrifice from those who are structurally and systematically powerless. Frederick Douglass—a social reconstructionist and democratic abolitionist—wrote,

> This struggle may be a moral one, or it may be a physical one, and it may be both moral and physical, but it must be a struggle. Power concedes nothing without a demand. It never did, and it never will.[3]

Political pundits and social commentators would have us believe that the protests, demonstrations, assemblies, and riots alike that erupted across the country in 2020 (amid a global pandemic, with folx risking their lives doubly) were centrally a response to American police brutality, particularly the murders of George Floyd, Breonna Taylor, and Ahmaud Arbery. Yet, the idea that the largest protest in American history is merely a response to police brutality is a fable meant to pacify white consciousness and the routinely American scapegoating of its aberrant identity. The protests we experienced, and continue to experience, are rooted in and born out of our dystopian fatigue with whiteness and the suffocation of our humanity when white supremacy strengthens its knee on our neck. As folx from all corners of existence—fleetingly unified by America's moral inequity and what Eric Foner describes as the "unresolved legacy of emancipation"—filled the streets, documenting the memory of Black bodies sodden in blood, their protests were not an answer, but a question. James Baldwin—a passionate and radically humane voice and writer who invited us to navigate Blackness, Americanness, and queerness—articulated *the* question with poignancy and precision:

> You always told me it takes time. It's taken my father's time, my mother's time, my uncle's time, my brothers' and my sisters' time. *How much time do you want for your progress?*[4]

Protesting in the spirit of such a large question, the question of how much time we must wait for social progress toward the ideals of life, liberty, and the pursuit of happiness for *all* folx, we must not feign astonishment when this question yields violence. The philosophy and praxis of violence as a sociopolitical mechanism within protests and protest rhetoric in defense of, or opposition to, the status quo as a marker of American public life has long been employed by white folx, while explicitly denied to Black folx, Brown folx, and nearly all non-white folx in this country. The founding of this nation, the *American Revolution*, spanning eight years, four months, and fifteen days of violence wrought to establish legal and economic independence from the British Empire.[5] The brutal four years and twenty-seven days of the *Civil War* superficially addressed the enslavement of Black people across the seceded Confederate states. White settler-colonialism has leveled still-unended centuries of genocidal cruelty against Indigenous Americans, purloining the land, imperializing the culture, and mass-killing millions of people. Violence of all sorts—physical, sexual, social, cultural, economic, spiritual, and more—drove Black chattel slavery from the moment the first enslaved Africans were displaced to Virginia in 1619. As Kellie Carter Jackson notes, "If violence is a political language, white Americans are native speakers. But Black people are also fluent in the act of resistance."[6]

In December 1866, Douglass penned an essay for *The Atlantic* in which he reflected on the benefits and burdens of Black resistance, a word which aptly encapsulates acts of protests. He poignantly wrote, "The thing worse than rebellion is the thing that causes rebellion." As such, for educators—Black educators—teaching has been, and remains to be, a response to and rebellion against a primary cause, white America's nativist compulsion toward violence. Violence against Black captives, many of whom were children and teenagers, wholesaled on the Western shores of Africa, trafficked across the globe, and enslaved in these United States of America as chattel for labor and sex. Violence of Black bodies hanged from trees with blood staining the crevasses of bark and dimming the bright pigment of plantation grass. Violence against Black men who, across Texas in 1865, neglected to "tip his hat" or "get off the sidewalk to let someone pass," and were casually murdered for these perceived violations of white supremacist etiquette.[7] Violence in Elaine, Arkansas, in September 1919, against nearly 200 Black sharecroppers who were murdered at the hands of American soldiers by the order of Governor Charles Brough. Violence on busses, before water fountains, and at lunch counters in the name of Jim Crow. Violence against Emmett Till, a 14-year-old Black boy, who was tortured, lynched, and mutilated for allegedly whistling at a white woman in Money, Mississippi, while visiting from Chicago in August 1955—only a year after the Supreme Court declared segregation in public schools unconstitutional, a decision which would have direct, though gradual, impact on young people his age across the nation. Violence in the bombing of the 16th Street Baptist Church in Birmingham, Alabama, in September 1963, killing Addie Mae Collins, Cynthia Wesley, Carole Robertson, and Carol Denise McNair—four little Black girls all aged fourteen. Violence claiming the lives of 648 Black folx in 1978, through mass murder/suicide, at the conspiracy-laced directive of James Warren Jones. Violence in 1991 against Rodney King by police who repeatedly struck him with more than 33 blows of a weaponized baton, orders from former Sergeant Stacey Cornell Koon to "hit his joints, hit the wrists, hit his elbows, hit his knees, hit his ankles." Violence in the murder of 17-year-old Trayvon Martin in 2012 on the basis of his "suspicious" appearance, adorned in a hoodie, walking from 7 to 11 with a bag of Skittles and an Arizona watermelon canned drink. Violence of a forced-entry apartment raid by the Louisville Metro Police Department, whose officers killed Breonna Taylor, a 26-year-old Black woman, with six bullets in the hallway of her home.

> *Against a canvas of violence, we taught.*
> *Against a canvas of violence, we teach.*
>
> *Against a canvas of violence, we continue(d) to believe in a star-spangled banner*
> *smudged by the ashes of the scorched dreams*
> *of those whose souls were / whose souls are stoned at desks with pencils*
> *made of the oak from which their ancestors hanged.*

Against a canvas of violence, we continue(d) to believe in a hope unseen, unheard, and unfelt, only known to us by a glimmering dance playing hide-and-seek
in the recesses of the eyes
of those whose souls were / whose souls are wearied from thirsting for the currency
made of cotton picked with splintered hands.

Against a canvas of violence, we protested.
Against a canvas of violence, we **protest.**

Yet, many teachers—of all races, ethnicities, gender and sexual identities, socioeconomic statuses, years of experience, and academic backgrounds—would neglect to think of and talk about themselves as protestors, or even protest-conspirators; and consequently, neglect to think of and talk about our classrooms as sites of protest, in part because of the dismal framing and negligent correlation of protests—when experienced as an assembly of Black bodies—equaling riots, riots equaling violence, and violence equaling "anti-American," particularly in this era when Black bodies are murdered at the hands of police, disproportionately impacted by an expansive pandemic, and the experiencers of unjust and subjugating economic, food, housing, criminal-legal, and educational conditions, acts of violence in and of themselves, thus the incarnated American paradox. But as the aforementioned undoubtedly determines, violence is as American as the flag itself. Thus, the aversion—intentionally or unintentionally—from educators toward the idea of seeing themselves as protestors and seeing our praxis as protest is erroneously skewed.

In a way, this isn't surprising. Teachers, who tend to prefer the reassurance of predictability, controllability, and respectability, protest as a sociopolitical tool and pedagogical mechanism is anything but predictable, controllable, or respectable—and therein lies its moral capacity to advance society's espoused ideals toward equity and justice. What we often neglect to confess as educators, either because we lack awareness or we are anxious about the implications, is the *proximity between* the politics of an inclination toward predictability and the politics of sustaining the status quo. Protest is risky. Protest rhetoric is dangerous. Embodying a protest ethic within our pedagogy compels us, as educators, to lean into the wisdom of William Lloyd Garrison, the white abolitionist and ally of Douglass, who said—

> I am aware, that many object to the severity of my language; but is there not cause for severity? I will be as harsh as truth, and as uncompromising as justice ... I am in earnest – I will not equivocate – I will not excuse – I will not retreat a single inch – AND I WILL BE HEARD. The apathy of the people is enough to make every statue leap from its pedestal, and to hasten the resurrection of the dead.[8]

We could hold to safe pedagogy. We could maintain the status quo in our classrooms. We could teach standards without substance. We could placate our propositions of race and racism for white respectability. We could ignore the identities of our students. But only, and I do mean *only*, the riskiness and danger of teaching as protest can advance the democratic ideals of this nation, realize the unresolved legacies of emancipation and justice, and reshape the narrative of what it means to be human(e) in an inhuman(e) nation. Only the riskiness and danger of teaching as protest can make real the possibilities, dreams, and hopes of our students by "the practice of imagining and pursuing a new world, a new way, and a new witness."[9] In this time, we must recover the moral arc of our work as teachers, as shapers of a nation, as formers and informers of a generational consciousness. It is not elective, it is requisite.

The question, then, is how do we rethink, reimagine, and ultimately *overhaul* our teaching as a moral enterprise and position it to be a practice of protest, thus emancipating our classrooms to become sites of protest and protest rhetoric as we conspire with students to call an empire—American whiteness—to task, and hold a political system—American democracy—accountable for its promises? How do we position what we do daily, for at least 180 days per year, to be a public praxis of protest tools of justice, guiding our classrooms through racial reflection while casting and creating a hope of what can be?

To start, there is something *within us,* as educators, to be recovered. Turn to the storied past of educators, namely Black educators from the early 1900s migration from South-to-North, and you'd discover something that once existed, a pedagogical pastime predating integration, something to be revived not in its original state but in a reclaimed and reimagined state. This particular imaginative moral ethic, latent within the fabric of many of our Black pedagogical ancestors, demands schools and classrooms in *this* time and of *this* moment to be full of folx with a common spirit, common mindset, and common aims struggling together for an awakened consciousness of pedagogical possibility.

What, you might be asking, is this imaginative moral ethic we must reclaim? It is an unwavering resoluteness to see and realize our teaching as an act of radical reverence born of the soul, rejecting the shallowed accumulation knowledge to sanctify individualism—which actively perpetuates competition in a flagrantly capitalist, ableist, militarist sense—both within and between individuals and communities; fueling, instead, the exceedingly, abundantly envisioned hopes that hallow knowledge as improving the public good. As the mother of grassroots citizenship education, Septima Clark, a formally trained educator at Benedict College and Hampton University—who was initially barred from teaching in Charleston, South Carolina—utilized her imaginative moral ethic to teach young people during the day in the classroom and adult literacy at night. By creating innovative methods, as a means of *protest*, to teach adults to read and write using mundane materials like a Sears catalog, literacy provided a pathway for citizenship education, which advanced access to voting rights, which emerged as democratic accountability. As a tool of resistance and creation, she believed, "knowledge could empower marginalized groups in ways that formal legal equality couldn't."[10]

That is, the imaginative moral ethic of pedagogy and protest offers us, as educators, the ability to see our work and our classrooms anew—within the dust of the chaos of Americanism and lived human experience, as a social motive in preparing young folx, namely Black and brown students, to experience knowledge as a means of liberation from the narrow utility of individual advancement, and a space in which we can reimage and expand the possibilities of what our communal society can be for *all folx*. The radical reverence of teaching as protest liberates the human spirit from knowledge as the sustenance of "what about *me*," and invites the human spirit to experience and make meaning of knowledge as the crux of "what about *us*."

Dr. W.E.B. Du Bois, a graduate of Fisk and Harvard Universities and known as a sociologist, historian, socialist thinker, Pan-Africanist, and professor, wrote in 1903 of the dangers of knowledge for narrow individualism in the pursuit of the social progress,

> …Atalanta is not the first or the last maiden whom greed of gold has led to defile the temple of Love; and not maids along, but men in the race of life, sink from the high and generous ideals of youth to the gambler's code of the Bourse;[11] and in all our nation's striving is not the Gospel of Work befouled by the Gospel of Pay? So common is this that one-half think it normal; so unquestioned, that we almost fear to question if the end of racing is not gold, if the aim of man is not rightly to be rich. And if this is the fault of America, how dire a danger lies before a new land and a new city … For every social ill the panacea of Wealth has been urged, —; and finally,

instead of Truth, Beauty, and Goodness, wealth as the ideal of the Public School.[12]

With dismay Du Bois' cautionary tale still holds true. Wealth is still seen as the panacea of all social ills, including the inequity and injustice of public schooling. Yet, since his writing, the wealth of this nation has been futile in repairing, reconciling, and emancipating our classrooms, though it reigns supreme.

Mrs. Tayborn once told our class, in a Du Boisian analysis at the intersection of knowledge and wealth in American communal identity,

> I don't care whether you're Black, white, Asian, Hispanic, or Indian, or some combination of all of 'em, you need to know about the green—the money—and how each and every one of you exists in a nation that's shaped by it, controlled by it, inspired by it, and, yet, ignorant about it. And based on what you learn during our time together, and what you do with what you learn, and how you decide to make meaning with what you learn, you will either play within that ignorantly inspired system of wealth and take advantage of it, or you will infiltrate it in order to protest against it, and by protesting it, I mean to make it better. Not better just for you and your folx, but better for others. People you've never met and never will. But people who are relying on you to make it better.

Therefore, if we are looking to render the classroom a space of what Paulo Reglus Neves Freire calls consciousness-raising, it is critical for us to look toward the imaginative moral ethic of protest, which transcends wealth and its supremacy in American capitalism. By inviting our students to protest the oppressive impositions of the world and experience knowledge as an *us over me* paradigm, the primary concern of the classroom becomes *a*rtistic, *i*lluminative, and *m*oral—constructing the acronym, *aim*.

With our aim cast forward toward an equitable and just nation we have yet to realize for Black and brown students, we bend our teaching from resistance to creation by cultivating racially conscious pedagogical approaches. By intention, production, implementation, and evaluation, these approaches, or stratagems or gambits, intentionally decenter whiteness—again, to be clear, not the skin color nor the actual folx who situate their ancestry in Europe—but whiteness, the supremacist structure of Americanism. They take up the challenge of centering Blackness—Black lives, Black lived experiences, Black identities, Black histories, Black cultures, Black voices, Black stories, Black imaginations, and Black possibilities. They cut deep through the white-hegemonizing, mass-industrializing, Common-Core-standardizing, quantitative-data-centering, creativity-repressing approach to teaching, which reifies "the banking conception of education," and which intentionally threatens the liberation of a student spirit to "transform that structure so that they [students] can become beings for themselves."[13]

This book offers a stock of racially conscious approaches, theoretical and pragmatic, to examine the ways in which we must conceive of our pedagogical imagination as a long-enduring series of protests that, in inquiry—the questions, theory—the ideas, and praxis—the acts, keeps society moving, growing, and progressing toward the realization of emancipation for Black and brown bodies, minds, hearts, and souls. In effect, it explores the idea of teaching as a protest in which the classroom itself becomes a permitted-by-proxy site of demonstration—perhaps the *most* quintessential action by which America's racial consciousness and, consequently, communal life has been shaped from generation to generation. By conceiving of protest as something greater than a function of particular sociopolitical movements throughout American history, *Teaching as Protest* casts pedagogy as a sociopolitical stratagem in itself, one that centers teaching—and those who teach—as key actors in forming and informing the future of America's democratic consciousness and racial equity. By centering teaching in its own right as a sociopolitical tool, teachers as actors and classrooms as stages are thought and talked about for their critical importance in influencing identities: individual and collective; and the ways teachers and classrooms mold the character of communities, restructure the communal landscape of what it means to hold America accountable for its espoused ideals of equity and justice, and advance an actualization of freedom that transcends individualism and radically reveres *community* as the highest virtue of regenerating the moral tissue of social progress.

If this book is philosophically rooted in a sociopolitical proposition of teaching as one of the core mechanisms, if not *the* core mechanism, for constructing learners' identities and learning communities toward justice-leaning ideals, its pragmatic approach will explicitly situate each racially conscious pedagogical approach in a *what-why-how framework*. Simon Sinek, a noted leadership theorist and thinker, popularized the concept of a Golden Circle, an organizational theory model that postulates how to present and communicate a value-proposition. Sinek uses neuroscience to explore how we are more apt to receive and embody knowledge when its communicators address *what* (the actual doing or providing), *how* (the ways by which "the what" is accomplished), and, most importantly, *why* (the purpose and reason, which triggers our limbic brain's processing of feelings of trust and loyalty).[14] This book incorporates this model while recognizing that what-why-how, an essential metacognitive strategy for all meaningful teaching, both antedates and transcends Sinek's application. While not utilizing what-why-how language explicitly, each approach will be unambiguously labeled in two subsections: *protest-in-context* and *protest-in-practice*.

Each chapter introduces its racially conscious approach—expansively, but not exhaustively—as a distinct mechanism for teaching as protest, not a sequential cumulation. Each approach opens with a why—a statement of purpose grounded in historical or personal narrative as informed by Black literary tradition and social theory. From the why, we flow into the what and the how. In emphasizing praxis—the language, tactics, and implementation of "teacher moves" (a phrase that this book seeks to reclaim from its hazardous cooptation by drive-through teacher mobilization programs, corps member organizations, and summer-preparation institutes), such as whole group prompts, accountable talk, higher-order questioning techniques, chunking information, and anticipating misconceptions—each chapter is meant to expand the way teachers think about, talk about, and teach about race, racism, racial consciousness, and racialization. As a matter of situating the content, I have taken the lead on *protest-in-context*; and my colleague, Susan, has taken the lead on *protest-in-practice*. The personal narratives which enhance and deepen each of the approaches, then, must be read through our individual lenses.

More expressly, the what and the why within each approach will be analyzed through a *being-doing* lens. This ensures that teachers approach the tool recognizing that there must be identity and mindset work—*being*—that precedes, and is continuously in conversation with, practices and modalities—*doing*. That is, this book argues for a particular mission of the classroom. At the intersection of pedagogy and protest, knowing how "to be," is experienced by seeing one's self, one's being, and one's becoming as ends unto themselves that transcend one's acting, one's doing, or one's producing. A knowledge of being is core to navigating society *human(e)ly*, demanding society to be accountable *human(e)ly*, and advocating for a more equitable society *human(e)ly*. These are all *human* acts, accessible to each of us as inherently good within the acts themselves. And these are *humane* acts because they consider the lived experiences of students within the classroom and strive for a beneficent community in which identity and identity-formation is invited and modeled through nonviolent, nontoxic, nonfixed risk-taking. To neglect, underprivilege, or even equate the significance of being with doing not only creates a transactional teaching experience that reinforces oppressive pedagogy, but also neglects the spirit of protest, which is integrally about the persons protesting and their embodiment of the protest more than the actual outcomes.

This is not to suggest that pedagogical-protestors—educators who see and experience their teaching as radical reverence for resisting individualism in order to advance equity and justice as the markers of social progress—ought to disregard outcomes. They should, however, evaluate a student's expanded and deepened knowledge of their being as the outcome of outcomes, and therefore as the product of protest. Through the looking glass of being-doing, the what-why-how framework invites teachers, along with the instructional leaders who coach and manage teachers, to explore three guiding questions: Who are we as protestors in the classroom? What will we do in our classrooms through our planning, preparation, and teaching to emancipate student being, thinking, *and* doing? And how will we refuse to perpetuate the systemically unjust, racist status quo?

Protests are vehemently about issues—social, political, theological—and function as an evocative mechanism to make those issues accessible and salient to the public, fueling the public to "speak truth to power." For the Ancient Greeks, *parrhesia*, the idea of truth-telling to those who were holders of power and privilege, was not only a rhetorical strategy, but was regarded as a moral duty, compelled out of a commitment to justice.[15] Michel Foucault, a French historian and philosopher who weaved critical thought between medicine, the social sciences, philosophy, and literature, notes of *parrhesia*—

> Parrhesia is a kind of verbal activity where the speaker has a specific relation to truth through frankness, a certain relationship to [her] own life through danger, a certain type of relation to [herself] or other people through criticism (self-criticism or criticism of other people), and a specific relation to moral law through freedom and duty … parrhesia is a verbal activity in which a speaker

> expresses [her] personal relationship to truth, and risks [her] life because [s]he recognizes truth-telling as a duty to improve or help other people ... In parrhesia, the speaker uses his freedom and chooses frankness instead of persuasion, truth instead of falsehood or silence, the risk of death instead of life and security, criticism instead of flattery, and moral duty instead of self-interest and moral apathy.[16]

For the Greeks, frankness, danger, (self) criticism, and duty toward freedom were the pillars of parrhesia. In what I call *pedagogical parrhesia*, I would contend that we bend the arc from protest as resistance to protest as creation to add *deep hope* as the fifth pillar. Dr. Andre C. Willis, a philosopher of religion and critical theory, says of deep hope,

> It is a generous, present disposition towards the future. It is an outgrowth of despair, not its enemy. We're thinking about a relationship to the present in a particular kind of discipline as one faces the present ... hope that is not an aspiration, it's not a probability, it's not a future orientation. It's a grounded-ness in the present facts of existence.[17]

Of utmost important in Willis' proposition is that our teaching must be "an outgrowth of despair, not its enemy." Those of us who are sensitive and responsive to despair, particularly in classrooms of Black and brown students, economically vulnerable and unhoused students, and students from all manners of socioeconomic and sociopolitical oppression, may risk sliding into a lamentable and traumatizing disposition. This despair-sliding oft happens with well-meaning white educators who are so ignorantly underexposed and uninformed to the lived conditions of what it means to be Black in this nation. Hence, the cultural myth of "white fragility" threatens to calcify despair within white educators who lack the lived experience of systematic subjugation—by the supremacy of the state and its individual enforcers. They've never had to cultivate a "generous, present disposition towards the future" because their everyday disposition is greeted with democratic generosity in this nation. Consequently, in the presence of Black despair—perceived or real—white educators tend to opt for "fragility" because it lacks the agency, urgency, or potency of hope for social progress. In the classroom, our teaching is a form of *parrhesia*, a moral rhetorical activity that demands frankness, danger, criticism, duty, and deep hope in order to invite our students *into* issues of inequity, injustice, and imbalanced power in order to give them the tools to speak truth to power. At the heart of this idea, *pedagogical parrhesia*, is an imaginative hope that young people—who are intrinsically the cleverest and freest truth-tellers, until coopted by the shallowed respectability politics of adulthood—possess the kind of radical democratic force necessary to not only hold our republic accountable, but also actualize its ideals for all citizens.

Instead of developing "criteria for success" to set our learning intention(s), let us reject the intimation of "success," steeped as it is in a production-yielding capitalist empire, and develop clear, coherent, and cogent criteria for *transformation*. Here, then, is how to approach and assess *pedagogical parrhesia*.

1. The teaching is *frank*, meaning it avoids any kind of veil that distorts the essence of what is being thought and talked about; instead, it uses direct language and accessible expressions—developmentally appropriate and trauma-sensitive, of course. As my grandmother, Olivia, would often say, "Say what you mean, and mean what you say. Don't leave folx guessing." In accordance with frankness is vulnerability, which suggests that, in order to be frank, one must also be vulnerable—defined here as the willingness to accept the risks of exposing one's self.

2. The teaching is *dangerous*, which is not to suggest a literal danger to the teacher but a danger to any systems of injustice and inequity. It is a willingness to risk likeability and diminish one's own power, privilege, or popularity in order to address any thought, word, or deed that intentionally or unintentionally underprivileges or subjugates folx, particularly Black folx. In accordance with danger is courage, which suggests that, in order to be dangerous, one must also be courageous—defined here as the willingness to do what causes fright within.
3. The teaching is *critical*, distinct from dangerous in that the criticism is connected to a particular thinking or doing. As danger is to a system, criticism is to an individual or a community. Practically speaking, criticism—of self or others—says, "this is how I am thinking and acting and how you are thinking and acting, and this is *why we should not* be thinking and acting in those ways." It is a human-centric mechanism. In accordance with criticism is humility, which suggests that, in order to be critical, one must also be humble—defined here as the refusal to put one's self higher than the community.
4. The teaching is a *duty*, signifying that it transcends external coercion and is only embodied and executed out of a sense of internal moral obligation. An educator who is coerced by a leader to reject oppression and move toward antiracism in the classroom does not use *pedagogical parrhesia*. But if the educator voluntarily does so out of a sense of internal moral obligation, then she performs a *pedagogically parrhesiastic* act. In accordance with duty is freedom, which suggests that, in order to be dutiful, one must also be free—defined here as the willingness to act apart from coercion.
5. The teaching is *hopeful*, not shallow hope which equates longing for equity and justice as one longs for the timely arrival of a delivery; instead, a hope that intentionally

invites one's self and community to be present as a practice of gratitude, without that gratitude becoming complacency. Hope, in this sense, sees despair not as an end, but as a means to an end, the ultimate fulfillment of the democratic ideals of this nation. It is a hope that is unafraid of *someday not being today, or even tomorrow*. In accordance with hope is empathy, which suggests that, in order to be hopeful, one must be empathetic—defined here as the willingness to replace one's point of view with another's, namely one who is suffering injustice.

As a form of protest, the truth-telling pedagogical process marks a distinction in how we usually think and talk about the pedagogical relationship between teacher and student. In *pedagogical parrhesia* as protest, both the teacher and the student struggle together, in community, as means of discovering, sharing, and reinventing truths about themselves and how those truths advance a common good for the oppressed and marginalized within American communal consciousness and communal life. At the same time, *pedagogical parrhesia* enables the teacher as much as the student to dispel and dismantle racist, biased, and oppressive thought—about identities, communities, politics, economics, and social safeties, which has been "exploited by dominant vested interests"[18]—while concurrently creating and/or accessing radically moral truths about race, racism, racial inequity, racialized framings, and racial hegemony. Bending the arc of protest and pedagogy does not happen alone, nor does it happen serendipitously. It happens by the force of teachers and students *as a result of and within* the community in which it is trying to advance.

For those of you who might be tempted to read the words "by force" as a call for diabolic, violent engagement, please eschew that interpretation. Instead, read it as a means of provoking change for the public good by weaponizing knowledge—questioned, doubted, critiqued—as a mechanism of *force de résistance* and a tool of democratic creativity. Force, then, in *pedagogical parrhesia* is a rhetorical weapon that will either usher students to maintain the status quo or abolish it. Or, as my grandmother, Alma, would tell me and my cousins when she heard us thoughtlessly and laxly communicating with each other, "watch what you say, because your words will either build something up or burn it down." As protestor pedagogues, the words we use are forces, and those words will either fortify this democracy and its racist, inequitable ways, or they'll resist what is in order to create what can be.

Before hundreds of attendees at the 1843 National Convention of Colored Citizens in Buffalo, New York, Henry Highland Garnet said, "No oppressed people have ever secured their liberty without resistance."[19]

Mrs. Tayborn dressed impeccably, the product of a cultural era that took seriously the intricacy of one's attire, particularly for Black women, as a kind of unspoken introduction in public life. My grandmothers, Alma and Olivia, were of that era. Both were born before our economy collapsed during Great Depression—Alma, 1920 in Tupelo, Mississippi, and Olivia, 1926 in Tunica, Mississippi. Both moved northward to St. Louis, Missouri, during first Great Migration of Black folx from the South from the 1910s to the 1940s, as they left behind sharecropping lands and agricultural responsibilities in pursuit of the industrialized social and economic possibilities of the big city. In a sign of their social and economic participation, Black women who'd become northerners were mostly seen in work uniforms and casual clothing during the week—tweed and cotton utility skirts and buttoned blouses with padded shoulders. On the weekends, they eloquently flaunted their skirts, dresses, and blouses of varying pastels and striped or floral designs, adorned with strands of pearls either fresh or faux, and walked in heels. Like so many others, Alma and Olivia leaned into a commonplace, unwritten, unspoken fashion dictum for Black women, which necessitated reserving their best, boldest, and most beautiful fashions for when they "stepped out" into the public domain—whether church, weddings, funerals, dinners, the movies, or even more informal social gatherings. They wore furs, cinched-in waists with full and billowing skirts, rounded shoulders, tailored jackets, and boasted pleating. For some, it was an exaggerated display of simplicity and modesty. For others, it was an exaggerated display of opulence and allure. As granny Alma once quipped to me, "When I thought I'd see white folx, I'd do a little more than usual. They weren't going to hold what I was wearing against me. They'll look for anything to have the upper-hand." Both women dressed as a form of dignity. Dressed as a form of respectability. Dressed as a form of accessibility. Dressed as a form of accountability. *Dressed as a form of protest.* Mrs. Tayborn dressed as a form of dignity. Dressed as a form of respectability. Dressed as a form of accessibility. Dressed as a form of accountability. *Dressed as a form of protest.*

Throughout middle school, I evaded physical education. Rather than sweat profusely, break the crease in my pants, undo my necktie, and the like, I chose instead to spend time with Mrs. Tayborn. Sometimes this meant having (a second) lunch, running errands in the building, or casually conversing in her classroom. I would do the same with Mrs. Martha J. Christmas—our school's counselor, and another Black woman of my grandmother's era—in her office. Inez and Martha were to the formation of my pedagogical identity as Alma and Olivia were to the formation of my human(e), socio-moral, and theological identity. You might think that educators, products of an era of respectability and accountability, would bridle at the thought of permitting me to evade a class. But they didn't. Much like my grandmothers, both Mrs. Tayborn and Christmas remarked regularly on the mutual joy, knowledge-sharing, and meaning-making that occurred during our spontaneous, informal gatherings. It is clear, in reflection, that they valued the intergenerational vibrancy of companionship with an inquisitive, voluble Black boy who was "an old soul," as oft remarked; and I valued their sagaciously frank, morally imaginative storytelling and their radically human(e), dangerously welcoming, and ethereally patient way of seeing, hearing, and understanding me, even when I failed to see, hear, and understand myself.

Mrs. Tayborn and I were having lunch one day, and I gathered that she was likely going to "step out" after school, because she was dressed-to-the-nines, even more dignified than usual, which was tough to surpass. With her dignity came a type of solemness that was palpable but not repellent. On the surface, it was a seemingly usual lunch of teacher and student. Underneath, per usual, there was something stirring within that I wanted to discuss with her—racism. Not racism in the systematic, heinous, white insurrectionist way as I know it now. But racism in a pre-teenage, individual, and sloppily unbecoming way. She obliged. It started with a white girl, Taylor, in my grade. She was my initial, conscious encounter with "white fragility" before we had that rhetoric for it. (Taylor reminds me that this rhetoric should be reserved for 10-, 11-, and 12-year-olds, since applying it too far beyond pre-adolescence is nothing more than excusing [conscious] white denial or white idiocy.) She was the embodiment of multifarious microaggressions, and even macroaggressions, who befriended mostly Black girls—friendship in the cursory, shallow, and cultural-appropriation sense—but often bawled nescience when confronted on her nefarious racial insensitivity by the very folx she called, "my girls." This particular day, after an exhaustive back-and-forth about a group assignment, she told me that I could "kiss [her] *white* ass." About an hour after, she apologized.

While I do not recall accepting her apology (though I certainly might have), I wanted to understand the ease with which she told a Black person, with whom she had a minimal relationship beyond a mutual grade level and classes, to "kiss [her] *white* ass." I recounted the conversation, for Mrs. Tayborn as we were leaving her class. She smirked, initially, then pursed her lips and sighed deeply, before nodding her head and casually but assuredly uttering, "Of course she did." A child of an era when she was the target of far harsher and more vile statements, you would think that being told to kiss someone's "white ass" would fail to warrant the emotive response she issued. But it was immediately evident that it was because she lived a history of language-induced, language-triggering trauma that those four words from Taylor resonated. While the entirety of our conversation escapes me, one distinct part of our conversation lives with me.

"Why did you say, 'Of course she did'? As if you're not shocked," I remember inquiring.

> Because I am not shocked. And you shouldn't be, either. A belief in white superiority often begins as a moment of what feels like white inferiority. And white inferiority often shows up as simple-minded. And what do simple-minded people do?

She rhetorically asked. "They say simple-minded things. And those simple-minded things, when left unchecked *by us, and definitely by their own*, becomes superiority-minded things."

I recall understanding the latter far more deceptively than the former but wanted to understand both. "What do you mean by, 'a belief in white superiority often begins as a moment of what feels like white inferiority'?"

"Let's walk," she said, because other students had started to gather where we were sitting. "When you questioned and doubted her within the group, those are acts of what?" Again, another rhetorical moment.

> Protest! Those are acts of protest. The same ones we've been using. She didn't know how to handle that. And why didn't she know how to handle that? Because, I assure you, her momma, daddy, grandma, pastor, or somebody tells her how smart she is and how special she

is. And what did you come along and do? Tell her the exact opposite of all she's likely heard. So she experienced the feeling of being *inferior*, and, in feeling inferior, she had to defend her superiority in the only way she knew how. So she told you to kiss her rear.

I nodded, understanding what Mrs. Tayborn meant, and also knew that I had not intentionally tried to make her feel inferior. In the context of what we had been tasked with completing, she was plainly amiss, and we were not going to suffer on account of her ego. "That wasn't my intention."

Who said it was? Who said it had to be? Who said anything about you? Feelings of white inferiority are not about you, me, or anybody else other than who? White people themselves! And they'll use anything, and I mean anything, to defend their honor, from how you show up in a group assignment to how you show up at the polls to how you show up in what you wear. Let me tell you something. You think I dress up to teach just because I like it?

This time, she looked for an answer.
"Yes ma'am … no ma'am … I don't know. Possibly." It was the best answer I had.
She continued, fierily.

On one hand, I do. I've always liked clothes. On the other hand, I dress up to teach because teaching is more than a profession. *Teaching is my protest.* And protests are performances. If I walked in here with my pajamas on or my head looking a mess, what might that do to my performance? It might risk it being seen, heard, trusted. So I put on clothes to protest in the classroom as actresses put on clothes to perform in the theatre. Their clothes compel us as an audience to see them; and my clothes compel white folx to see me. And even now, I'll be in a store and a white saleswoman will start experiencing self-scripted feelings of white inferiority. How will she try to defend her assumed superiority? By telling me the price! But whether it's in the classroom or in the store, you know what I do? I keep dressing up. I keep showing up. I keep telling my truth. I keep calling out the system. I keep shining light on lies. I keep teaching. And if I keep showing up, you keep showing up. If I keep telling the truth, you keep telling the truth. If I keep calling out the system, you keep calling it out. And if I keep teaching, you keep making meaning. Let white folx deal with being white.

Notes

1. Martin L. King, Jr. (1963). "I Have a Dream Speech," at the March on Washington for Jobs and Freedom, Washington, D.C.
2. Frank A. Thomas. (2018). *How to Preach a Dangerous Sermon*. Nashville: Abingdon Press, xxi.
3. Frederick Douglass quoted by Shawki, Ahmed. (2005). *Black Liberation and Socialism*. New York: Haymarket Books, 13.
4. Karen Thorsen, director. (1989). *James Baldwin: The Price of the Ticket*. PBS.
5. Maryland State House. (2007). "The Road to Peace, A Chronology: 1779–1784." William L. Clements Library, The Maryland State House. Retrieved on February 18, 2021 from: https://msa.maryland.gov/msa/mdstatehouse/html/road_peace.html
6. Kellie Carter Jackson, "The Double Standard of the American Riot." *The Atlantic*, June 1, 2020. Retrieved from: https://www.theatlantic.com/culture/archive/2020/06/riots-are-american-way-george-floyd-protests/612466/
7. Eric Foner, "Southern Violence during Reconstruction." *PBS*. Retrieved from: https://www.pbs.org/wgbh/americanexperience/features/reconstruction-southern-violence-during-reconstruction/

8. William Lloyd Garrison. (1971). "I Will be Heard, 1822-1835." *The Letters of William Lloyd Garrison,* vol. I, edited by Walter M. Merrill. Cambridge, MA: Harvard University Press [Belknap].
9. Robert S. Harvey. (2021). *Abolitionist Leadership in Schools: Undoing Systemic Injustice through Communally Conscious Education.* New York: Routledge, 18.
10. Brown-Nagin, Tomiko. (1999). "The Transformation of a Social Movement into Law? The SCLC and NAACP's Campaigns for Civil Rights Reconsidered in the Light of the Educational Activism of Septima Clark." *Women's History Review*, Vol. 8: 81–137.
11. A stock market, or economic trading system, in a non-English nation.
12. W.E. Burghardt Du Bois. (1903). *The Souls of Black Folks: Essays and Sketches.* Cambridge: University Press, John Wilson and Son, 77–79.
13. Paulo Freire. (2018). *Pedagogy of the Oppressed, 50th Anniversary Edition.* New York: Bloomsbury Publishing, Inc., 74.
14. Simon Sinek. (2011). *Start with Why: How Great Leaders Inspire Everyone to Take Action.* New York: Penguin Books, 39.
15. Michel Foucault. (1983). *Discourse and Truth: The Problematization of Parrhesia.* Lectures at The University of California at Berkeley. Retrieved from: https://foucault.info/parrhesia/
16. *Ibid.*
17. Andre C. Willis. (2017). "Life is Short, But It Doesn't Have to Be Shallow—How to Capture Deep Hope." *Los Angeles Hope Festival.* Retrieved from: https://bigthink.com/videos/andre-c-willis-deep-hope-how-capitalism-hijacked-our-emotions-to-sell-stuff
18. Jonathan Church. (2021). *Reinventing Racism: Why "White Fragility" Is the Wrong Way to Think About Racial Inequality.* Lanhan, MD: Rowman & Littlefield, 66.
19. Kellie Carter Jackson. (2020). *Force and Freedom: Black Abolitionists and the Politics of Violence.* Philadelphia: University of Pennsylvania Press, 15.

2
Disordered Attachments: The Risks and Revolution of Identities Work

Robert S. Harvey

Amanda was sitting in the food court of Terminal One in the Minneapolis-Saint Paul International Airport. She was a young, bright-eyed, 28-year-old white woman with five years of teaching experience. She lived in Tulsa, Oklahoma, only a mile away from the Greenwood District, more commonly known as "Black Wall Street." In 1921, over the course of two days, government-sanctioned mobs of white folx violently destroyed 35 square blocks of the Greenwood area, killing anywhere from 30 to 300, injuring more than 800, displacing more than 10,000 from their homes, and destroying more than 35 square blocks of businesses.

One hundred years after that vile demonstration of racial violence and white supremacy, Amanda and I found ourselves in conversation. It was March 2021, and I had just deboarded an early-morning, three-hour flight from LaGuardia Airport in New York City that departed at 6:00am Eastern Standard Time and was preparing for a long layover before a final flight to Memphis. While the flight from New York City was immensely

DOI: 10.4324/9781003183365-2

comfortable, our pandemic-restricted in-flight service permitted no meals beyond a ziplocked bag of water and cookies, creating that peculiar kind of hunger that inhibits cordiality—to say nothing of an unplanned conversation about race and racism. I was in line waiting for an everything bagel and a vanilla oat-milk latte. Perhaps because of the mask covering more than half of my face, Amanda was seemingly unaware of those inhibitions. She held a copy of *White Fragility*, which should be more honestly retitled *Whiteness: The Privilege to Feign Fragility and Avoid Accountability*. Standing behind a Black man catalyzed an unnatural amount of joy in her, relative to my hunger and sleepiness.

"Good morning!" she said, lowering her mask as if to disarm her greeting. While I was vaccinated by that time, a privilege of being an educator in New York City, her lowering of that mask still vexed me.

"Hi," I replied with about as much vigor as a lazy moth.

She responded, as if we were long lost friends, "So! Where are you headed?"

"Memphis. But, I didn't catch your name." I figured if we were going to have this waiting line conversation, we at least needed to exchange names.

"Amanda," she said, and followed with her last name. "I *freaking* love Memphis! I used to go there all the time for Memphis in May—have you ever been to that festival before? Oh my God … the barbecue!"

"My name is Robert. And yes. I used to live there for four years. I am headed back to visit an aunt." I then preempted her inevitable follow-up questions. "I live in Manhattan now, East Harlem, specifically. I moved in 2019 to join a network of charter schools."

> Love New York City! I mean, who doesn't? There's so much to do. So much to eat. So much to see. Oh! And so much diversity. I was raised in a small town in New

England, in Connecticut, so we didn't have much diversity at all. Just a bunch of white people.

Her framing of diversity was similar to me: limiting its expansiveness to the singular category of race, suggesting that all white folx are one category, and classifying all the rest of us as "diversity." I simply nodded. It was the easier of my options in that moment.

I work in education, too! Teacher. Five years. Elementary. Love *my* kiddos! I started at a new school this year, and I am loving it compared to where I was. My principal, whom I love—she's so unapologetic about who she is [often, though not always, code for 'she's Black']—has us reading this book.

She held up the book and asked if I'd like to see it. "Oh, no, thank you, I've read it," I replied.

"I'm not done yet, so I won't ask what you think about it. Don't want to spoil it for me!"

Again, I nodded. I heard a barista call my name and order, which felt, in a beautifully utopian way, like an ethereal rescue attempt from wherever this conversation about white fragility, her "unapologetic" principal, and teaching in Tulsa would lead us. As I proceed to reclaim the effervescent kindness and hospitality that is endemic to who I am, Amanda continued.

"You know what I love about this book so far?" she asked, waiting patiently for me to affirm intrigue.

I indulged, "What's that?"

After so many years, I can say it now—I'm white. Not Caucasian, not Italian ... even though my family is from Italy ... both sides ... none of those cover-ups to try to not take responsibility for what happens in this country. I'm white. So now that I can say that,

> I am just trying to be really, *really* honest with how white this nation is ... how white we are ... how white I am ... without making any excuses for why I am this way. So much of what I thought and how I acted, and even how I showed up as a teacher was because of my family, and the town I was raised in, and who I spent time with as a child, and where I went to school, and who my friends were, and where I went to college, and the church I attended, and even who I married. But those truths are no excuse for the ways I've treated people in the past, or even for some of things I probably say to my students now. I just hope they can be patient with me, like *really patient*, because I am so early on this journey that I know it's going to take years for me to get *it* right. However long it takes, I'm going to get it right. I have to. I want to. And I just know that the best lesson I can ever give my students is to focus on me ... *to work on me*. You know?

Pausing for a moment to assess how I might reply, I took a sip of my latte.

> I would contend, as a Black man committed to Black and brown children, and the work of freeing our classrooms from *all* oppressors and oppressive structures, that the best lesson you can give your students is to focus on dismantling your whiteness, working on your complicity with whiteness, and then guiding your students on how to navigate and deconstruct the very social construct that has shaped the fact that you have the privilege of assuming that Black and brown young folx owe you patience. Have a good flight and be well.

Less than two weeks later, I received an email from Amanda, simple and to-the-point:

> You were right, so right. Thank you. I hope you enjoyed your time in Memphis.
> —Amanda
>
> p.s. I am now reading, *So You Want to Talk About Race*."

What Amanda failed to realize in her identities-work is that teaching and learning, at its crux, is a communal endeavor, and to dissociate it from its communality is to pillage its function as protest, both philosophically and performatively. Moreover, by her use of teaching and learning for self-focused analysis— under the deluded guise that self-focused identities-work is "the best lesson" that she, as a white person, can give her primarily Black and brown students— Amanda embodied the disordered attachment of white selfishness, at great harm to the advancement of emancipation. I'll write more on disordered attachments later in this book, but, for the moment, I want to be clear. This is not an attempt to talk about selfishness in its infantile form of "give me back my toy," or "I was standing in line first" (though there is something to be said about whiteness and its implicit expectation for firstness!).[1] Rather, this is selfishness in the form of an exhaustive, self-centered, unending identities-work swan song intoned by white folx, particularly in Black and brown teaching and learning communities, whereby Black and brown folx are expected to yield patience as white folx discover their whiteness. It is a song I dismally call *the supremacist shadow of the indulged white self*. Classrooms, intrinsically, are intended to be sites of anti-individualism and the embodied refutation of self-focus. Upon crossing the threshold from hallway to classroom, students *and* teacher yield an I-consciousness and take on a we-consciousness; a kind of we-consciousness that considers the individuality of each "I" without any particular "I" overconsuming or monopolizing all of the space. Therefore, for a white woman to center the supremacist shadow of a "focus on me ... work on me" narrative as a fundamental cog of her teaching and learning is to reject the very communal proposition and we-consciousness of classrooms.

Paradoxically, America—the golden calf of whiteness—is, at its crux, pro-individual and anti-communal, thus privileging the I-consciousness in all of its systems and structures, namely in capitalism. Despite its pledged refrain of "one nation under God," the evidence of how it has historically regarded and continues to regard the majority of its citizens, particularly its citizens existing within the boundaries of non-hegemonic social categories—Black, Latinx, Asian, women, queer, economically vulnerable, unhoused, uninsured, unemployed, underpaid, neurodivergent, physically disabled, and incalculable other lived identities attempting to survive at the margin—would suggest that we are *many nations under gods*. But here's the critical detail. The petite-nation, in this country, which seems to be the most centered, protected, and feted, is the *indulged white self* and what it needs first before it can be concerned about what Black and brown folx need. This notion of the interconnectedness between racism, selfishness, self-interest, and identities-work has been considered across the spectrum of racial equity and abolitionist scholarship, from professor and historian of race Ibram Kendi in America to Thomas Sowell, a Black libertarian-conservative social theorist and economist—whom I disagree with the greater part of his socio-political and racial analysis. Tersely, Sowell writes, "While racists, by definition, prefer their own race to other races, individual racists—like other people—tend to prefer themselves most of all."[2]

When it comes to white folx committed to cultivating and living out a pedagogical ethic of protest, identities matter. Professor of philosophy and law Kwame Anthony Appiah forthrightly underscores why identities matter:

> ... they matter, first, because having an identity can give you a sense of how you fit into the social world. Every identity makes it possible, that is, for you to speak as one "I" among some "us": to belong to some "we." But a further crucial aspect of what identities offer is that they give you reasons for doing things ... not only does your identity give *you* reasons to do things, it can give others reasons to do things *to* you.[3]

Because identities matter, identities-work matters. Yet, the work of analyzing and unpacking one's identities—race only being one of many—has often been exploited by white folx as their *disordered attachment* in teaching and learning communities to evade the higher-order cognitive praxis of translating identities analysis into pedagogical reconstruction, thereby rarely achieving protesting-in-practice, and merely protesting-in-thought. For decades, social identity theorists have examined the impacts that social forces have on individual identities and, reciprocally, how these identities impact the way people show up within and navigate social structures and systems, such as teaching and learning communities. Because the social structures are complex, all of us classify ourselves and others into numerous categories in order to both simplify how we interact with each other and to make sense of who we are relative to those folx we are interacting with. Are they the oppressor, or are we the oppressor? Are they the privileged, or are we the privileged? Are we to be afraid, or are we the font of fear?

Social identity theory contends that individuals' identities are partially based on our relationship to varying social categories and our membership within those categories, particularly if those categories are socio-politically, socioculturally, and socioeconomically hegemonic—white, male, heterosexual,

Christian or majority religion, married, post-secondary credentialed, wealthy, homeowner, and so forth. Whether we are members within a hegemonic social category or not, all of us possess a set of social identities—e.g., male/female/non-binary, conservative/liberal/independent/apolitical, gay/lesbian/transgender/queer/asexual, working class/middle class/upper class, and countless others—and utilize these identities, intentionally and unintentionally, within our classrooms to distribute, make meaning of, and assess knowledge, manage (or police) bodies and behaviors, and/or curate a power-politic between ourselves and our students. Most conspicuous of all social categories is race. Within the historical American context of race and racialization, there is a particularly charged oppressive/oppressor binary between Blackness and whiteness that is as present and prevalent in teaching and learning as it is in every other social and cultural space within this nation.

Against the backdrop of the last decade as America's delinquent racial reckoning has moved center-stage since the murder of 17-year-old Trayvon Martin in 2012 in Sanford, Florida, Black and brown folx have had to listen, *ad nauseam*, to putatively well-meaning white folx, like Amanda, talk about the identities-work they were pursuing as an effort to see and understand their whiteness. Though ample encounters prove that white folx rarely are compelled to think of themselves as possessing a racial identity, social theory suggests that,

> When the dominant status of whites relative to racial and ethnic minorities is secure and unchallenged, white identity likely remains dormant. When whites perceive their group's dominant status is threatened or their group is unfairly disadvantaged, however, their racial identity may become salient ...[4]

Now, with hundreds of millions of people across the globe challenging the social, political, cultural, and economic dominance of whiteness, there are hundreds of thousands, possibly millions—key word, *possibly*—of white folx who are now realizing what Black and brown folx have known all along: they're white. As white folx recognize their whiteness from the site of classrooms and teaching and learning communities, their pedagogical parrhesia must include an indisputable abdication of any kind of identities-centeredness that neglects to see the work of understanding the pedagogical influence of our identities only as an antecedent to *what happens* in the classrooms. That is, identities-work must be a means to an end, and not an end unto itself. For many, this will require a psychological excavation of the *selfishness and egotism* that is socially entangled in the lived construct of white supremacist culture; and require the dismantling of the normative assumptions of how white folx assess "getting it right." What is right is not a realization of whiteness. What is right is protesting one's whiteness as part of, but not the entirety of, protesting whiteness within teaching and learning, thus emancipating Black and brown kids from the structural oppressions built on and maintained by whiteness.

One of the dangers of this specific type of selfishness as an extension of white identities-work is that it habitually yields guilt. Guilt instinctively centers heavily internalized emotions that risk allowing white folx to fully deflect from *how to* be racially non-violent, particularly in their teaching and learning, and subsequently deflect from *how to* alleviate suffering as a result of their actions in classrooms. Instead, their identities-work becomes all about their feelings of guilt, and they psycho-strategizing amongst themselves to get rid of the uncomfortable feelings associated with that guilt. In a study about white guilt and its responses to racial inequities, Iyer, Leach, and Crosby contend that white guilt consistently proves itself to be a self-focused, self-centered, egotistical emotion, which "leads to an overriding concern with making restitution to the disadvantaged."[5] Consequently, the guilt of white identities-work tends to yield quick compensatory actions. These might include half-hearted apologies and performative pedagogical antics, rather than deeper systemic action: consistent antiracist and racially conscious commitments, curriculum and assessment overhauling, redistributions of power, or even restructuring instructional planning and execution. In that sense, the feelings borne out of identities-work that white folx, particularly white educators, tend to favor are but another incarnation of white supremacy's preoccupation with itself. Thus, Blackness—the social construct of oppression—falls into invisibility.

It is for this very reason why "white guilt" is not only problematic as a notion for racial consciousness identities-work, but prohibitive to bending the moral arc of pedagogical parrhesia, because rarely does guilt yield frankness, criticism, danger, duty, and hope. Instead, guilt yields a disinclination, on the part of white folx, to analyze and/or associate their habitual disposition of self-centeredness as a part of their socialized identity. Our dispositions without analyzation are what French sociologist Pierre Bourdieu called our *habitus*.[6] For Bourdieu, habitus is a "set of dispositions to respond more or less spontaneously to the world in particularly ways, without much thought," because our habitus is seeded into us—as if it is natural—by those who participate in raising us.[7]

> Parents tell you not to speak with your mouth full, to sit up straight, not to touch your food with your left hand, and so on, and thus form table manners that are likely to stick with you all your life. Once they are inculcated, these habits aren't consciously associate with an identity: middle-class English people don't consciously decide to hold their knives in their right hands in order to act English, any more than Ghanaians use only their right hand to eat in order to display that they're Ghanaian. But these habits were nevertheless shaped by their identities.[8]

In the same manner, guiltiness and selfishness is such the habitus of white identities-work that it habitually [pun intended!]

subsists without critical analyzation. This is, in part, why radical calls for pedagogical protest at school, district, state, and national levels diminish in momentum: the ephemeral moments of Black suffering and oppression are eclipsed by white habitus—the selfishness of white folx—needing time to come into the knowledge of their whiteness and its devastating impact on society. To be clear, feelings-informed identities-work, when formed and informed on the basis of pedagogical accountability and emancipatory praxis, can function as a steppingstone—sure. It may even be *the initial* stone toward accountability and praxis. As poignant and intimate as they may be to the individual, the feelings that result from identities-analysis can conceivably prevent white folx from scapegoating racialized oppression as something of "those people." Think about the number of white folx who created an intra-race binary between themselves and the January 6, 2021 Capitol insurrectionists. Guilt, as a result of coming into the knowledge of whiteness, invites "good" white people and "those" white people into the same conversation of whiteness. Through those feelings, individuals who acknowledge their identities in proximity to whiteness—and how that whiteness infiltrates schools across this nation—are better positioned to pedagogically protest centuries of dispossession, aggression, and oppression, and the continued social-emotional and intellectual violence occurring on the lands of schools from "sea to shining sea." The guiding question, then, is: what are white folx going to do with the feelings of all that identities-work? Will those feelings translate into pedagogical parrhesia, institutional restructuring, compensatory overhauling, power redistributing, data-reframing, and community-based advocating? Or will those feelings merely yield more feelings?

In American teaching and learning communities, unregulated, selfishness-yielding identities-work peaks at the intersection between whiteness and democracy. Here, innumerable white educators seem to believe that their pedagogical protest is limited to and defined by their ability to become aware of their whiteness; and, for the exceptional ones, to become aware of how their whiteness yields a selfish disregard for the Black and brown students within their classrooms. This selfishness cyclically reaches its peak every time an innocent Black body is murdered by the nation's white supremacist "blue privilege,"[9] when white folx escape into the hallowed privacy of affinity spaces to make sense of our national pastime—racism. These spaces, while oft used in meaningful ways for the facilitation of challenging dialogues without pretense or fear of judgement from *the other*, can dangerously become baleful sanctuaries for white folx to feign their grief. This, while "not understanding what they expect us to do about it. It's not like we're the ones who are racist out here doing that kind of stuff," as one white teacher shared with me after the killing of Ahmaud Arbery. This *supremacist shadow of the indulged white self,* unintentionally—and, in its most dangerous form, intentionally—reifies a kind of self-centered individualism, which whiteness has always been about. Ultimately, the swing of the long arm of individualism reaches and bruises the noses of Black and brown and queer and economically vulnerable students, who oppressively become victims of their teachers.

At the other end of this spectrum are the white educators who, at the expense of their students, have embraced a caricature of pedagogical protest absent identities-analysis, passively performed using black boxes on their Instagram feeds, Facebook profiles, and other social media, new wall posters of iconic Black and brown public figures and lesser known images of the #BLM movement, Black-created music as a call to community circles, t-shirts adorned with "Black Lives Matter" and "Trust Black Womxn," door-threshold fist bumps with catchy phrases, and off-rhythm melodies to introduce learning objectives and make cross-content connections. Are these practices at the hands of white folx inherently caricatured? No. Are these practices at the hands of white folx inherently problematic? No. Are these practices at the hands of white folx inherently racist? No. Being one with the culture of the times, a micro-dimension of an antiracist and abolitionist pedagogy, is necessary for radical teaching and learning protest to take place. And yet, for white folx, being one with the culture of the times demands not caricaturing the times as a form of *shuckin' and jivin'*, thus pedagogically subordinating Black and brown students to make sense and make meaning of the possibilities of protest because their white teacher has not journeyed within before journeying outwardly.

For these practices to be meaningful forms of pedagogical protest for white folx, they must begin with an internal consciousness of whiteness. That internal consciousness, when probed intently, will inevitably yield the radical centering of the histories, significances, virtues, and voices of Black and brown folx. Minimally, it will catalyze white educators to think twice, and thrice, before engaging in appropriating, a staple practice to white supremacy culture in this country. Assumedly unbeknownst to the white folx at this end of the spectrum of selfishness, performative protest, specifically through signs and symbols that demonstrate little-to-no evidence of identities-analysis, is a type of evasive dismissal of Black humanity and racial consciousness, in that it yields an illusory naiveness that "we are one in community" on the basis of learning and appropriating a culture's communal anthropology. This is why pedagogical parrhesia, namely for white folx, demands a self-critique as much as it does a critique of systems, because folx who want to protest well must first begin within by protesting the ways they have become complicit with and/or pawns of both ends of the spectrum of the *supremacist shadow of the indulged white self*. In the work of antiracist and abolitionist teaching and learning, progenies of pedagogical parrhesia, the supremacist selfishness of white folx, in their exhaustive, unending identities-work, is itself a pandemic, one experienced unequally along race and class lines, with economically vulnerable Black and brown young people bearing the brunt of the pandemic.

In classrooms from New York to Biloxi to Chicago to Chattanooga to Atlanta to Little Rock to Denver to Albuquerque to Oakland to Seattle, the extent of a visible and conscious pedagogical protest has been limited to the identities-work of white educators wrestling with: "Who am I? What are my conscious and unconscious biases? Why are these my biases?" Do those questions have a modicum of value in classrooms? Sure, because there is an individual, introspective praxis to developing a pedagogical parrhesia that ensures a classroom of resistance and emancipatory creation for all students, particularly Black and brown and Indigenous American students. Nonetheless, those questions risk white folx slipping into the deflection-slide of the *supremacist shadow of the indulged white self* that conflates self-growth as being equally as consequential as pedagogical protest. This pandemic of white selfishness, borne of colonialism, has made the transformative and hopeful possibilities of a new, equitable, and human(e) praxis in our classrooms far more distant by delayed inaction—while white folx in affinity groups, professional development workshops, and virtual webinars, come to terms with being white—and will eventually punish Black and brown students in the ways it always punishes Black and brown students, through social-emotional and intellectual violence and shifting the emancipatory responsibility within the classroom onto Black and brown minds. The good news is that we know what light we need to turn on within our classrooms to absolve the *supremacist shadow of the indulged white self*: a pedagogical parrhesia that maintains the emancipation of all oppressed folx—abolition—as its highest ideal, and acquiesces to communal consciousness as its elemental antidote for white individualism.

The *supremacist shadow of the indulged white self* is directly connected to difficulties of "giving whiteness up" as an imperative of pedagogical protest, framed out in the previous chapter. Divergent to the idealistic assumption that we regularly espouse the costs of selfishness to children, for white folx, in fact, selfishness is the cheaper moral option. Imagine that. Meanwhile, a communal consciousness that forms and informs white folx acting as a moral agent on the behalf of emancipation is costly—and not just costly, dangerous—to whiteness. In some ways, this is obviously true even to those who would argue against it; people who are committed to redistributing their power, privilege, and possessions in order to realize a more equitable world will be required to distribute less to themselves, therefore *costing* them. And, on the other hand, people who selfishly act in ways that prioritize their interests above all others are expensed of nothing. But, on the premise of identities and identities-work, does this argument still hold? Of course. Privileging one's identities-work, as a white person, over and above the pedagogical parrhesia that emancipates classrooms for Black and brown young people is the cheaper of the options—when you are the moral subject and therefore the focus of *your* pedagogy.

On the contrary, privileging pedagogical parrhesia as the catalyst of emancipation without forcing Black and brown students to become the bearers of your identities-analysis is costly and dangerous—for you. Costly, because it demands that you sacrifice the need for a perfected analysis of your whiteness in order to ensure that the students who call you "teacher" experience a classroom wherein their freedom, meaning making of knowledge, and hopes about the world are centered over your quest of self-discovery. Dangerous because it requires you to decenter whiteness, which risks decentering all you know, or assume to know, about "getting it right" when it comes to teaching and learning. The variable that we must explicitly name and situate here is that the cost-analysis of identities-work selfishness or communal consciousness is the more costly pedagogical pursuit hinges on who we define as the moral subject of the classroom. When you—the white educator—are the subject of the classroom and the pedagogy within it, it is cheaper to be selfish in your pursuit of identities-analysis. But, when the students, particularly Black and brown students, are the subject—not object—of the classroom, your identities-analysis is the costlier of the options because it is being charged against the emancipation of those young people.

As white folx stall their transition from the *disordered attachments* of their individual identities-work, "for however long it takes," to systematic and structural pedagogical work in classrooms and in teaching and in assessments and in learning, Black and brown students are colonialized into mere tools being leveraged in white folx' pursuit of being better white folx. To some of you, this entire claim might read impractical, unworkable, or even counterintuitive, particularly if you are guided by the premise that white folx must decipher and deconstruct *all* of their problematic mindsets and methods *as a prerequisite to* shifting their pedagogical practices. Instead, white folx, through intentionality and accountability, must avoid getting stuck in the identities-deciphering and deconstructing work as a prerequisite to more equitable, justice-leaning, and human(e) teaching. The guaranteed way to retain status quo pedagogy is to sanction white folx to pursue indefinite self-focused identities-work. Pedagogical parrhesia maintains the emancipation of all oppressed folx—abolition—as its highest ideal and acquiesces to communal consciousness as its elemental antidote for white individualism, including the self-centered identities-analysis that has consumed center-stage in DEI workshops, antiracist breakout rooms, and professional development sessions.

In effect, identities-work for white educators becomes their end in the emancipation of the classroom. Meanwhile, Black and brown educators must do identities-work *and* translate that work into a classroom praxis that realizes deconstructed curriculum, increased representation, balanced assessments between the quantitative and qualitative, centering the voices and lived knowledge of the marginalized, and yield metrics deemed proficient for sustained employability. For so many white educators, their identities-work is solely an attachment that provides them with a means of transcending or evading accountability. For so many Black educators, our identities-work is the postern by which we transcend identities being our sole attachment, but rather identities as a means to pedagogical parrhesia.

On this idea of attachments, I look toward Ignatius of Loyola, a Spanish theologian and Christian mystic, one of the leading figures in the Roman Catholic Counter-Reformation of the sixteenth century, and founder of the Jesuits, who wrote most lucidly about *disordered attachments*. For Ignatius, these are the things to which we are so attached to that they keep us from becoming a person who embodies and lives out the highest version of ourselves in *and* for the world. To some degree, he thought of these disordered attachments as *unfreedoms*, because we are so attached to these particular ways of thought and being that they both prevent us from freely acting in ways that enhance the world, and rationalize the ways in which we oppress others who are not in alignment with our disordered attachments. In ancient orthodox theology, an attachment is "an emotional dependence, either of one person on another, or of a person on some real or illusory object."[10] For white folx committed to cultivating pedagogical parrhesia, their infatuation with *the supremacist shadow of the indulged white self* is a disordered attachment to an illusory form of protest—because it is, in fact, an attachment to themselves; and that attachment to themselves becomes the rationalization by which they oppress Black and brown students. It is seldom, if ever, a vehement, maleficent attachment to the self, i.e., "these Black and brown kids are going to have to wait for me to figure me out first." Instead, it is ordinarily a subtle, sympathetic attachment to the self, i.e., "I just hope they can be patient with me, like *really patient…*" Because of this disordered attachment to centering themselves and their identities-work, white educators "consequently make an end of the means, and so what they ought to put first, they put last."[11] How, then, do folx committed to pedagogical parrhesia surmount disordered attachments? Ignatius proposed, in Latin, *agere contra*. Agere means *to act*, and contra is *against*—"to act against." Edward Lo, a Jesuit scholar of contemplative life, has described *agere contra* this way:

> We can be attached to patterns of behaviour that seemingly make us feel safer, be they our insecurities, doubts, or unwillingness to be pulled out of our comfort zones. Agere contra helps us to confront those things that hold us back from such freedom; better yet, it helps us to grow into this freedom.[12]

For Ignatius, we deconstruct and dismantle complicity with disordered attachments by acting in ways and doing those things that transcend our disordered attachments—even though those things, initially, will feel *unnatural* to us. In the systemic framework of American whiteness, a self-focusedness is natural, which means that white folx acting against their own self-focusedness is the *agere contra*, and for many, that is unnerving because whiteness and its domination of Black, brown, oppressed, and vulnerable bodies subsists "on making the end fit the means."[13] Not just *the* means, but *their* means. But to act against the *supremacist shadow of the indulged white self* is to act against the natural inclination of pedagogical complicity, thus spurring a form of protest within the classroom whereby identities-work is subordinated as a means to the end. Not just *any* end, but *the* end that bends the moral arc of justice toward the good for Black and brown and oppression and vulnerable students. By identities-work becoming a means to bending that moral arc, thus creating an emancipated democracy where freedom, justice, and equity are available to and the benchmark for *all* students—all means all—then, white folx can become pedagogically parrhesiastic educators.

To transition into this next section, I'd like to start with a poem, "Who Said It Was Simple," by Audre Lorde. You can read the poem on the Poetry Foundation's website by using a smartphone to scan the accompanying QR code.

Disordered attachments in identities-work are not only the encumbrance of white educators attempting to do pedagogical parrhesia (or white folx in general). But in fact, they are also, invariably, the burden of Black and brown folx. The attachments are polarly distinctive, but each poses their own unique, destructive risk for students. For Black educators, there is a particular enthrall with a race-centric approach to pedagogical parrhesia, as when our race becomes the *solitary* point of departure in our protest ethic. It is as if, for many Black and brown folx, our oppression-consciousness, and equally so, our power-consciousness, are limited to and restricted by how we are oppressed and/or how we access power exclusively on the basis of race. This constricting race-only pedagogical parrhesia risks creating a classroom context whereby we guide our students in teaching and learning to only name and situate their racial identity—or in globally migrant framing, their color—as the only means of oppression and power. Thus, the *agere contra* for Black and brown educators, in particular, is to rebuff a race-only pedagogical parrhesia, and instead, espouse an intersectional pedagogically parrhesia. An intersectional framework invites a *race-first, but not race-only* approach.

A trusted colleague and friend of mine made, in conversation, a counterargument to this proposition, which will likely be the default retort for many readers: does not a race-first approach jeopardize pauperizing the very real, complex, historical realities of race and racism in this country into just *a* form of oppression equal to others? The obvious answer is *possibly*. The less obvious answer is *not necessarily*, because the impact of any pedagogical approach pivots on the educator implementing the approach. The overall problem, however, with the counterargument that we must maintain a race-only approach until we have dismantled whiteness as to not dilute the impact of racism, is that many of our students—explicitly our developmentally younger students—lack the cognitive capacity, and *duly so*, of compartmentalizing their social identities for the sake of adult analysis. As sociologist Patricia Hill Collins notes of Kimberlé Crenshaw's coined term, *intersectionality*, our students are wrestling with the "interdependent phenomena" of their social oppressions, whether based on race, gender, sexuality, socioeconomic class, (dis)ability, nationality, or any other social category. In effect, our student's oppressions and *our* oppressions cannot be deftly compartmentalized as all of us attempt to circumnavigate our lived human experiences in the abyss of the supremacist shadow of America's indulged white self. Consequently, to justly place race and racism on the block for deconstructive analysis in its proximity to oppression and power, we—Black and brown educators committed to an emancipation of all of our students—must be committed in our pedagogy to look at how race intersects with, forms and informs, nuances and gradates other social identities-markers.

In "Who Said It Was Simple," Audre Lorde—Black, woman, and lesbian—modestly and elegiacally, wrestles with the intersecting experiences of these oppressive dimensions of her witness in the world. She probes and scrutinizes herself as a divided-being at risk of "shatter" because of the anger borne of the weight of her intersecting oppressions. She opens the first stanza, "There are so many roots to the tree of anger/ that sometimes the branches shatter/ before they bear." Lorde, in this succinct exposé at the intersection of racism and sexism and homophobia, provides a somber, but droll truth that most of us can understand. While she penned these words in 1973, they could have been written in 2003, or today, or in 1897. In fact, the roots of which she writes, were quarried in 1897 by W.E. Burghardt Du Bois—

> It is a peculiar sensation, this double-consciousness, this sense of always looking at one's self through the eyes of others, of measuring one's soul by the tape of a world that looks on in amused contempt and pity. One feels his two-ness, — an American, a Negro; two souls, two thoughts, two unreconciled strivings; two warring ideals in one dark body, whose dogged strength alone keeps it from being torn asunder.[14]

From Du Bois to Lorde, both educators in their own rights, and now to us—Black and brown educators committed to pedagogical parrhesia—we must introduce and situate intersectionality for students to make sense and make meaning of hundreds, if not thousands, of years of oppression: denial of basic human dignity because of social categories. To not utilize intersectionality in our identities-work, analysis, and pedagogical parrhesia in order to maintain what Crenshaw calls a "single-axis framework,"[15] we carelessly and prejudicially erase crucial, defining elements of our students' identities. In other words, race-only identities-work from Black and brown educators endangers our classrooms of becoming discriminatory communities whereby students disregard core social categories in order to respect the power politics guiding the context, a politic that often is shaped by our prejudiced categories. Even more notably to the Black and brown dilemma of identities-work is that when elect a race-only pedagogical parrhesia, we are intentionally subordinating—whether we acknowledge the intention or not—the other social categories that make us who *we* are in our teaching and, even more complexly, inform our positions of power as the facilitating leader within the classroom. When we consider the pedagogical consequences of this dilemma—intentionally subordinating how our *other* social categories inform our proximity to oppression and/or power—there are very few sustaining counterarguments against a critique of race-only pedagogical parrhesia. To ensure that this claim is not unduly appraised as being metaphorical, let me be clear: the pedagogical protest—

> of a Black male is distinctive from a Black female
> of a Black transgender woman is distinctive from a Black cisgender woman
> of a Black American-born person is distinctive from a Black migrant
> of a Black neurotypical person is distinctive from a Black neurodivergent person
> of a Black queer person is distinctive from a Black heterosexual
> of the Black working class is distinctive from the Black upper-middle class
> of a Black baby boomer is distinctive from a Black millennial
> of a Black Christian is distinctive from a Black Muslim
> of Black rural folx is distinctive from Black urban folx
> of Black first-generation college folx from Black legacy-institution folx

My most proximate lived experience of intersectionality as critical to pedagogical parrhesia is in navigating classrooms and education leadership as a Black, male, upper-middle class person. To enter into the classroom and implement instruction that frames any sociocultural, sociopolitical, or socioeconomic issues as merely a race-only issue would neglect the power dynamics within myself as the educator guiding the classroom. Take, for example, a discussion around American healthcare inequities and accessing quality medical care. While Black folx disproportionately suffer from higher rates of hypertension, diabetes, and obesity—a racially universal evidence of inequity—Black cisgender women and transgender women endure compounding inequities as a result of sexism and gender oppression in this country. With all of my we-consciousness, ignoring my closer proximity to healthcare privilege that I maintain solely on the basis of being a male would not only be negligent to the pedagogical process, but immoral. Immoral, because any failure of my part as a Black male to acknowledge, admit, and analyze the privilege of my maleness relative to women in the receipt of quality medical care is, in fact, my complicity with upholding patriarchy and male privilege, each of which are manifestations of sexism. Moreover, intersectional identities-work demands that within this pedagogical moment, I acknowledge and situate what it means to have and access health insurance, which compounds proximity to privilege in a nation where more than 32 million residents, under the age of 65, are uninsured.[16] In our identities-work as Black and brown educators, we must discuss the history, systems, and biases of sexism, homophobia, classism, and other isms and phobias that contribute, in manifold ways, to understanding the complexity of oppression within a shared racial community. In sum, Black and brown identities and oppression on the basis of racial identities are much broader than the universalization of Blackness that most of our pedagogical protest provides. Yet, the continued insistence of a race-only filtering for our pedagogical parrhesia within classrooms guarantees that Black and brown students who live at the intersection of multi-marginalization are obscured from being seen, heard, understood, advocated for, or emancipated.

What is particularly challenging about this proposition is that it will require Black male folx, like myself, who are proximate to privilege on the basis of gender and/or gender performativity, to first be honest about our proximity; and secondly, to deconstruct the ways in which we use our proximity to that privilege in our pedagogy—and, more pointedly, in our daily lives. In 2010, sociologist L'Heureux Lewis quite simply called this, "Black male privilege," which he clearly denotes as being relative to Black women, not relative to whiteness. Situating his argument in the social plight of mass incarceration, he says—

> If we think about the narrative of mass incarceration, we think about the ways in which black men and black boys have been locked up at increasing rates since the 1980s. While this is true, the fastest growing incarceration rate is particularly among black and Latino/x women. And because we haven't thought seriously about what's happening with black girls and Latino/x girls, we tend to make the issue of incarceration solely male, and we miss the different ways in which we need to be intervening not just for our young boys, but also our young girls.[17]

Some folx, namely Black male folx, have argued that feminist and womanist uses of the idea of Black male privilege fails to take seriously the sociopolitical plights of Black men within the historical narrative of American whiteness; and how Black men have seemingly been the brightest target, literally and figuratively, of America's state-sanctioned weaponized violence. To that end, Black men arguing against the validity of our privilege morphs our identities as Black men into a disordered attachment whereby we rather hold tightly to the unfreedom of Black women, who must navigate the compounding compression of situating race *and* gender in their identities-analysis. Furthermore, speaking personally from the sociopolitical location of being a Black male, when we are unwilling to acknowledge our privilege relative to women and therefore "deny both the unique compoundedness of their situation and the centrality of their experience to the larger classes of women and Blacks,"[18] we are furthering uncritical, patriarchal, dominant ways of thinking and being. More poignantly, I am rejecting the unique compoundedness of folx like my Black mother, my Black aunts and cousins, my Black friends, my Black colleagues, and the landscape of Black women who have participated in, and still working toward, creating an abolitionist democracy for me and other Black men. At one end of reading this proposition there will be Black males who contend like one educator told me,

> I don't see why you want to pit us against Black women like we're their *biggest* oppressor. Come on now, man! You can't possibly tell me that when it comes to white people and all of their stuff against Black women, then comes to us [meaning Black men], we are as problematic as the white people. Most of us are fighting the same enemy they are. I don't buy it!

On the other end of reading this proposition, there will be Black males who do the revolutionary identities-work necessary to walk toward the emancipation of Black women through an embrace and internalization of the tenets of feminism and womanism. This end of the spectrum will be complicated, because it will demand of Black male educators that we actively utilize our classrooms to sacrifice our privilege by centering the stories, voices, lived experiences, tragedies, triumphs, and sociopolitically unique compoundedness of Black women. Furthermore, this end of the spectrum will be complicated, because, while most of us as Black males are conscious of our Blackness, our maleness in the world is often implicitly navigated—it just *is* without interrogation—and, therefore, typically not seen, analyzed, or discussed at all either among ourselves or within broader conversations around Black oppression and privilege. Despite the complicatedness and the identities-work it will require of Black males to deconstruct the tightly confined oppression consciousness with which we maintain the privilege to engage, we must do the work. Failure to do so marginalizes Black women *and more particularly*, Black women educators, within our schools and classrooms, thus reifying patriarchy in the minds of our students; and it makes the pedagogical parrhesiastic goal of emancipation even more difficult to realize. This proposition is not restrictive to gender and/or gender performativity. It must extend to any and all forms of compounded oppression within Blackness. That said, this passage was acutely about gender because of the ways in which male privilege has historically exercised its dominance over women within Blackness; and has abused the compassionate morality and categorical supportiveness of Black women for our own advancement. Equally, this was about gender because of the ways in which we can conceal many of our other social categories; a concealing that is not cooperative for an emancipated classroom, but a concealing that is often encompassed as a dual-tool of safety and naming-resistance. That is to say, we can often conceal our sexualities, socioeconomic classes, familial histories, and political identities as resistance mechanisms to reclaim power from a white supremacist ethic that often demands that Black and brown folx disrobe and expose ourselves on the auction block of "inclusion." Dissimilar to those categories, gender is often inferred, and thus holds a markedly weighty identities-analysis.

If any real efforts are to be made within classrooms to advance pedagogical parrhesia that envisions, hopes for, and realizes the emancipation of all oppressed folx—abolition—as its highest ideal, and acquiesces to communal consciousness as its elemental antidote for white individualism, then it must include intersectional identities-work for Black and brown educators. It will be an uphill climb, but the title of Lorde's poem aptly poses the rhetorical question we must hold to in the difficulty of that climb, "who said it was simple?"

Notes

1. Charles Sanders Peirce, a pragmatist philosopher and logician, coined the phenomenological idea of *firstness* to denote, "an instance of that kind of consciousness which involves no analysis, comparison or any process whatsoever … it has its own quality which consists of nothing else. Charles S. Peirce, Charles

Hartshorne, Paul Weiss, & Arthur W. Burks. (1960). *Collected Papers of Charles Sanders Peirce: Edited by Charles Hartshorne and Paul Weiss: Principles of Philosophy and Elements of Logic (Vol. 1).* Cambridge, MA: Harvard University Press, 152.
2. Thomas Sowell. (2019). *Discrimination and Disparities.* New York: Basic Books, 45.
3. Kwame Anthony Appiah. (2018). *The Lies That Bind: Rethinking Identity.* New York: Liveright Publishing Corporation, 9–10.
4. Ashley Elizabeth Jardina. (2014). "Demise of Dominance: Group Threat and the New Relevance of White Identity for American Politics" (Dissertation). University of Michigan, Ann Arbor, Michigan, 3.
5. Aarti Iyer, Colin Wayne Leach, Faye J. Crosby. (2003). "White Guilt and Racial Compensation: The Benefits and Limits of Self-Focus." *Personality and Social Psychology Bulletin*, vol. 29, no. 1: 117–129.
6. Pierre Bourdieu. (2020). *Habitus and Field, General Sociology, Volume 2 (1982–1983).* New York: Wiley.
7. Appiah, 21.
8. *Ibid.*
9. Willie Dwayne Francois, III. (2021). "Outing Blue Privilege: Police Criminality, the Necro-Theological, and the Struggle for Black Liberation." *Africana Race and Communication and Criminal Justice Reform: A Reflective Analysis of Adaptive Vitality.* Washington, DC: Lexington Books. *Manuscript in preparation.*
10. John A. Hardon, S.J. (1985). *Pocket Catholic Dictionary: An Abridged Edition of the Modern Catholic Dictionary.* New York: Doubleday, 34.
11. Michael Ivens, S.J., Translator. (2004). *The Spiritual Exercises of Saint Ignatius of Loyola.* Herefordshire: Gracewing, 49.
12. Ricj Mastroianni. (2019). "Agere Contra: Moving Against, Moving Toward." *Coracle Journal.* Retrieved from: https://inthecoracle.org/2019/10/agere-contra-moving-against-moving-toward/
13. Ivens, 49.
14. W. E. Burghardt Du Bois. (1897). "Strivings of the Negro People." *The Atlantic.* Retrieved from: https://www.theatlantic.com/magazine/archive/1897/08/strivings-of-the-negro-people/305446/

15. Kimberlé Crenshaw. (1989). "Demarginalizing the Intersection of Race and Sex: A Black Feminist Critique of Antidiscrimination Doctrine, Feminist Theory and Antiracist Politics." *University of Chicago Legal Forum,* vol. 1, Article 8: 140.
16. National Center for Healthcare Statistics. (2019). "Health Insurance Coverage: Early Release of Estimates from the National Health Interview Survey, 2019." *National Health Survey Early Release Program*, Center for Disease Control and Prevention, Released 9/2020, 1.
17. L'Heureux Lewis. (2010). "Black Male Privilege?" Interview with Michael Martin. *NPR News*. Retrieved from: https://www.npr.org/templates/story/story.php?storyId=124320675
18. Crenshaw, 150.

3

An Appeal to White Folx in White Spaces: What Are We Giving Up?

Susan Gonzowitz

Late on a Thursday night, after a long snow day filled with diapers, building blocks, too much hot chocolate, and an evening graduate class, I finally sat down to get some writing done on this chapter. Staring at the blank screen, I wondered what I could possibly say that someone else had not already said. I flipped through emails, went through some old text message exchanges, and finally asked my Afro-Latino husband, a career educator, "What do I want to say to white people?"

He pulled his face out of his book long enough to smirk and say, "I don't know what you want to say to your people. Stop being white?"

While he laughed, that is in fact what I want to say. *Racism does not cease to exist unless whiteness, as a social construct, ceases to exist.* Being an antiracist white person is not about what we give *to* the movement, it is about what we give up *for* it.

Since I entered the field of education, there has been no shortage of white practitioners marketing the next big thing in education. Books packed with decontextualized teaching practices

DOI: 10.4324/9781003183365-3

were passed out at every professional development and spread as the gospel for "getting kids to learn." As some of my veteran colleagues would joke, the next big thing often looked an awful lot like the big thing from ten years ago. That criticism led me to see that the ideas offered by these (frequently white) self-marketed change-agents were often freshly packaged practices that had been co-opted from effective Black and brown teachers. This pattern is not limited to high-visibility educators alone though. At one school I worked in, a 20-something white teacher started every day with his Black and Latinx students by leading a call-and-response chant. In my room down the hall we could hear desks being pounded on throughout the day. When I asked him about the practice, he told me "it gets the blood flowing and adds that joy-factor." He did not once reference the long history of call-and-response in Black American culture—from musical performance to religious practice, or even use its African roots as a historical marker for a teaching moment; he did not acknowledge the power of drumming in so many African and indigenous cultures as a communal means of communication, mourning, celebration, and hope. White educators are talented at appropriating an impactful practice, spreading the gospel, turning it into a movement, hollowing it of what made it work, and then blaming the practice when it fails; a cycle which is born of the legacy of colonialism. Antiracist teaching is at risk of becoming yet another bleached education practice. As white educators, it is our responsibility to recognize what antiracist teaching means for white folx in white spaces, and what it means for white folx who work in Black, brown, and Indigenous spaces. While antiracist practices are context-specific and there is not one formula for solving racism, all white educators must understand that whiteness is a culture, a political construct that takes over and dominates our teaching and learning spaces.

Educators of white children, in particular, should realize that at the root of this problem is how whiteness is transmitted from parent to child. As Margaret A. Hagerman points out in her book about raising white children, it is "important that parents think about the larger social environment that they construct for their children, thinking about what they *do* in addition to what they *say*."[1] So, to better understand my work, I once joined a white parenting group. My participation in the group lasted for about four weeks—as one of my professors, Dr. Shannon R. Waite says, "Know your work, sis!"—but in those four weeks, I learned quite a bit about how whiteness shows up in white parenting spaces, about myself as a white woman, and about my future work as a white educator. During one discussion about interrupting [micro]aggressions—a phrase that, without careful probing, can assuage whiteness of its impact on folx of color—parents were eager to get advice on how to couch the critical feedback they would offer their children after the kids committed aggressions. Parents offered one another sentence-starters.

"I know you never want to hurt someone, but..." one suggested.

"I know you intended that as a compliment, but..." another recommended.

After the third or fourth sentence starter, I asked if any of them was concerned that they were centering the feelings of the white child instead of the harm that was caused against the child of color. I suggested that grounding the feedback in the white child's emotions might inadvertently teach that child to consider their own feelings over the needs of the actual sufferer of the aggression. The other parents in the group thought the scaffolds created "an access point" for their children and would help "build resilience in the face of criticism." This approach, though, risks building a generation of self-centered white adults who are too brittle to engage in honest conversations about racism and the impact of their whiteness.

The desire to center an individual white child's well-being over anyone and everything else is a symptom of the greater *"me vs. us"* mindset pervasive within whiteness. Many of us are unwilling to understand that sacrifice is our greatest form of protest, and so we repeat the same racist patterns generation after generation, even as we claim to care about and pursue racial equity. Hagerman points to the mindset that "good" parents push "for resources for their own children, even if those resources are the result of the historical legacy of white supremacy in the United States."[2] The white flight of the 1950s and 1960s, combined with a long history of red-lining and discrimination in real-estate practices, ensured that white folx have disproportionately used local tax dollars to pump money into our own public schools and provide our students with better funded and traditionally higher-ranked education.[3]

In my own white community, where *Black Lives Matter* and *Hate Has No Home Here* signs litter lawns and racial equity committee members hand out flyers every Saturday, white mothers arrive en mass to public hearings to protest the development of affordable housing because of the potential impact on class sizes in the *public* school district. Community members have consistently expressed concern about the potential of adding 115–150 students[4] to a school district of roughly 3,800 students. One community member was quoted in the local paper saying, "that would put a tremendous strain on our school district. I do not believe that taxpayer-owned land should be rezoned for mixed residential buildings in our town."[5] At local Town Board meetings parents passionately present well-researched ["well" meaning time-exhausted and energy-expended], data-driven arguments about the loss of learning that students will experience if class sizes grow from 16 to 20 students and explain that they moved to this community for the "good schools," which, according to the *U.S. News & World Report's Best High Schools of 2019*, almost always translates to majority white schools.[6] Hagerman reflects that white folx,

> ... can learn to shift their own ways of thinking and acting in the world if they allow themselves to face the discomfort that inevitably comes with honest confrontations with race ... to accept that the potential collective benefits of

challenging forms of racism in private white spaces ultimately outweigh any perceived personal, emotional cost.[7]

To eliminate this need for individual comfort, I wonder what it might look like for white teachers who work with predominantly white students to create spaces where open conflict does not require "a spoonful of sugar to help the medicine go down"[8] and criticism does not lead to defensiveness. As Bettina L. Love points out in her essay *There is Nothing Fragile About Racism*, "After 13 years of schooling, many white students end their K-12 experience without ever having a teacher of color or being challenged to disrupt their learned racism."[9] I have only lived in my current community for six months and already see this pattern playing out. My two children went from a daycare that was almost all Black and Latinx teachers to one where I believe every single teacher identifies as white. Without my husband and I intentionally gearing dinner table conversations to issues of race and racism, my children would rarely have to think of their world beyond the white bubble they now find themselves in. When one of their teachers told us at a back-to-school night that sunscreen is required at any temperature because "students at this age have such fair skin," it was important for me to ask my five-year-old son if he thought the word "fair" was the right choice and to ask him how he thought I should talk to his teacher about the discrimination present in her word choice.

As a first step to figure out how to make interrupting a regular practice, I began Googling questions like, *"How do I know if I am being selfish?"* and *"Signs that I am defensive."* I found countless numbers of self-help sites and psychologist blogs that all talked about defensiveness being an impulse, not a choice, and a natural reaction to fear. So, I wondered, are there ways that white teachers can teach their white students to self-regulate; to catch themselves in their worst moments of impulsive whiteness and to course-correct? To do this effectively, white teachers would first have to recognize and define their own whiteness and analyze their relationships to it. When talking about the teacher candidate she worked with, Joyce E. King points out in her essay on dysconscious racism,

> Not only are they often unaware of their own ideological perspectives (or of the range of alternatives they have not consciously considered), most are also unaware of how their own subjective identities reflect an uncritical identification with the existing social order.[10]

White children cannot begin to practice empathy, the embodiment of imagining their lives in someone else's shoes, if they do not have teachers equipped to show them that there are other shoes to try on. For white educators living and working in white spaces, it may be easy not to accept or even see the "existing social order." Unlike white teachers who are working in Black and brown spaces, white educators teaching in white spaces are rarely asked to complete ethnographies and demographic landscapes of the communities in which they will serve. White teachers in white spaces are often not compelled to learn the culture of the community and are frequently given permission to ignore, remain blind to, or compartmentalize the whiteness that shapes our spaces; and so, as James Baldwin says,

> ... people who imagine that their histories flatter them are impaled on their history like a butterfly on a pin and become incapable of seeing or changing themselves, or the world. This is the place in which it seems to me most white Americans find themselves. Impaled. They are dimly, or vividly, aware that the history they have fed themselves is mainly a lie, but they do not know how to release themselves from it.[11]

If white teachers of white children were to educate themselves on the culture and history of their communities, they could discover why the community, the school, or even the tracked classes within the school are so segregated. They could learn the written and unwritten rules—sociopolitical tools of shaping culture—that historically kept our spaces white and discover the rippling effect of those practices and tools. Once white educators understand how our spaces are intentionally kept white, they will be better equipped to identify and disrupt the practices that maintain whiteness. Within our own classrooms, from the very first day of school, there are concrete strategies that white teachers can use to protest and disrupt whiteness.

In most teacher preparation programs, teaching candidates are taught to create classroom contracts or agreements with their young people; a set of rules to which students will all adhere in order to maintain order in the classroom. The very premise of these contracts, often used by white teachers in majority Black and Brown learning spaces, are a power intersection of capitalism, colonialism, and whiteness. Often, only the students' actions are policed in these contracts. Even in all-white spaces, the idea of reducing our behavior to a contractual agreement seems to undermine the humanity and sense of community we could help our students to value.

Aspiring teachers are taught to work collaboratively to make these contracts in a variety of ways, but the goals are always to create secure, inclusive environments in which students know and agree to what is expected of them. For white teachers working with white kids, this type of agreement can be reimagined as approaches of protest, and our ways of doing things can be reconstructed—ways that have been passed down to us and, consciously or not, perpetuated among us by white supremacy. Instead of a typical contract, it might be more effective to create an agreed-upon list of *What We Will Do Differently This Year*. There are a lot of useful tools for identifying white Western values, but I particularly appreciate the work of Tema Okun and dRWorks, because they offer a clear list both of cultural behaviors and of "antidotes" for those behaviors.[12] Imagine if, instead of "Always try your best, show respect for myself and others, etc.," a classroom contract had agreements like:

1. Instead of striving for perfection, I will set small, challenging goals for myself and my peers, celebrate my own growth, celebrate when others have done work I can learn from, ask for and give constructive feedback, and consider the success of my end product as a part of a longer growth process.
2. Instead of being defensive when something does not go as expected, I will name what makes me uncomfortable, find the good in what happened, consider other approaches carefully, and embrace a new approach or a compromise.
3. Instead of assuming that my teachers have all of the answers, I will look for knowledge in my peers, in media, and in other community members. I will rely on my teachers to ask me challenging questions, to help me when my thinking or computation needs course correcting, and to facilitate my learning.
4. Instead of thinking that there are right and wrong ways to do things, I will look for multiple pathways to success, question my peers' work to encourage divergent thinking, and celebrate when I find new ways to approach familiar problems.
5. Instead of seeking recognition for my individual accomplishments, I will recognize and celebrate the accomplishments of my classmates, seek peer feedback as a regular part of my work, and engage in team work as least as frequently as I work on individual tasks.

Agreements like these can become tools of protest if used to support students to develop an understanding that there is another way to be; agreements like these can invite students to empathy, which will allow them to question their own self-identities. As

King points out, "Any serious challenge to the status quo that calls this racial privilege into question inevitably challenges the self-identity of White people..."[13] And that's not a bad thing. Questioning our own identities, which we can do only once we have named and defined our own identities, will allow us the space to embrace what is best about other ways of doing and being. If each of these classroom agreements is carefully developed, rehearsed, and enforced, then students can learn to decenter themselves, to accept critique without feeling personally attacked, and to value repairing harm over the feeling of vindication. To make a list like this meaningful and to use it as a tool to decenter whiteness, I recommend the following steps with classes of white students:

1. **Define culture**

    There are many ways to define culture with students, but the definition I have found to be the most compelling is the one that my colleague, clinical psychologist Dr. Sherryl Browne Graves, has used each summer when we co-teach a course to prospective teachers. She explains to them that everyone has a *big 'C' Culture* and a *little 'c' culture*. Our *big C Culture* is the culture of our people: the music, the food, the style, the language(s), the holidays, the customs, and the values that we engage in with extended family and community. *Little c culture* is the culture of our home: it's what we eat for dinner and with whom we eat it, it's bedtime routines, it's stories and sayings we return to regularly, it's how we express love, and it's how we spend Saturday mornings. For more advanced students, teachers may also want to consider adding a third layer of culture—an even bigger, more all-encompassing culture that is ideological. This aspect of culture is the U.S. culture of oppression and privilege; for white children, this means recognizing the culture of privilege that allows them to move in their world without constant fear of being criminalized, rendered invisible, or undervalued.

2. **Unpack all of the cultures we have in our classroom**

   Once you create a working definition of culture, students can share stories and bring artifacts of their own cultures into the classroom. Some white students may have ethnic cultures to share, but others might find that, beyond the holidays they celebrate, it can often be easier for them to share evidence of *little c culture* than *Big C culture*. When this happens, we can support them to find *Big C Culture* by asking them how their community defines, celebrates, and honors success; we can ask them what magazines and commercials define as beautiful; we can ask them to consider what movies and music are awarded each year.

3. **Define white culture and identify-specific elements of white culture**

   Because, for many of us, whiteness has become a reflexive way of doing and being, it is often hard for young people to see it as a culture unto itself. But if we look at the collective list of *Big C Culture,* trends should emerge. There will be collective culture around family structure, worship, food, music, but most particularly around values. These white values, often called "American values," are our culture. The list will most likely include things like competition, progress, academic accomplishments, safety, security, perfection, etc. If you are struggling to generate a list of shared values, use a resource like the Tema Okun list and ask students to tell you if the ones you share are values that are reinforced in their lives.

4. **Consider the harm that white culture can cause when it is the only way of being and doing**

   Once you have the list of values generated, consider what it might be like to move in our world if you are someone who does not share these values or does not see their home culture reflected in these values. One of the most effective ways to do this is to read writings by Black folx about whiteness. James Baldwin,[14] bell hooks,[15] Alice Walker,[16] Toni Morrison,[17] Kwame Ture,[18] and Claudia Rankine[19] have all written essays on the topic. Outsider picture books can also help younger readers make sense of this experience. It is important for young people to begin to recognize that when we exclusively reward white values—because the white way is the "American way"—we cause harm to those who do not subscribe to white ways of doing and being. Students should consider how they would feel if their home language, their home foods, their family structures, their home values, or their histories were not represented in their daily school experiences.

5. **Select aspects of white culture that the class wants to protest**

    Once students engage in discussions on the damage that whiteness can cause, they are ready to think about which white norms they want to protest as the beginning of deconstructing. We are not telling students to forego their own culture, but we are requiring them to try on a different way of doing and being. For this year, in this class, we learn how to decenter our own whiteness and experiment with more inclusive practices. It will be hard for students to unlearn what they have known since birth, so select norms that most of the class agrees are worth challenging. If you do not have general consensus, the process will not work and you should spend more time on step four.

6. **Brainstorm "other ways of doing" in response to those aspects of white culture**

    It is not enough for students to decide that they want to try something differently. They must know what different looks like. They should play with sentence starters like:

1. "If I am not going to strive for _____ then I can _____ instead."
2. "If I am not going to celebrate _____ then I can celebrate _____ instead."

Students should brainstorm approaches, but if they need guidance, return to the work of Tema Okun.

7. **Make the agreement and practice the new ways of doing**

    Once you have the norms and have brainstormed alternative ways of being and doing, you are ready to create this new type of classroom agreement. Just as you would with any beginning-of-year agreement, generate your list of to-dos [affirming thinking and doing that are in alignment with protested and disrupted whiteness], share examples and nonexamples, give students scenarios and ask them what values they are or are not upholding, and then display the agreement somewhere where it can be referred back to regularly as a form of community-making.

8. **Celebrate when class community members protest whiteness and name when they do not**

    As with any new learning and particularly with unlearning, students will need time and patience as they develop these new norms. When you find students slipping into old mindsets and behaviors, you will need to reset, intentionally inviting the discomfort of unlearning. You will need to name what you see happening and ask them to try again. For example, if a student is upset about a grade, you need to remind them that they are not striving for perfection and prompt them, "Instead of being emotional about the grade, tell me what you learned from at least one corrected error on this test or from at least one comment on this paper." If a student hurts a peer's feelings and defaults to defensiveness, you need to encourage them to acknowledge that that reaction is not helpful because it cannot get to the truth of what really happened, nor is their reaction helpful to healing the harm done to the peer.

9. **Provide students with frequent, periodic growth-based feedback**

    We measure what we value. If you genuinely want students to internalize these shifts in behavior, you must give them feedback on their performance. When you sit down for report card conferences, you should celebrate growth, set growth goals, and acknowledge pain points just as you would in any academic area.

As we explored in Chapter 2, the work of actively decentering whiteness can often be stalled by teachers who become mired in their own identity work. As white educators work with white students, their *disordered attachments* in teaching and learning communities can interrupt their pedagogical reconstruction. The fear of doing the work wrong or of causing insult can make it easier for white adults to avoid reconstructing teaching and learning spaces.

In order to situate our methods in a more universal context of being, curriculum needs to be grounded in a truth that decenters the whiteness that is always centered. Besides interrupting whiteness in daily interactions in our classrooms, it is also important for us as educators to unearth whiteness in our resources, approaches, and strategies. To do this, we should scrutinize not just the books in our libraries, the pictures we hang on our walls, but also the stories we tell, the rubrics we use, and the context of curriculum and pedagogy. I recommend the following protocol, which can be used with teacher learning groups or directly with older students:

1. Facilitator Describes the Item/Protocol Using the Following Guiding Questions:

    a. Whose voices contributed to the creation of this item or protocol?

b. What research was taken into account in the creation of this item or protocol?
c. How much did context influence the creation of this item or protocol?
d. In what ways were stakeholders of this item or protocol involved in its creation and implementation?
e. How was this item or protocol tested with stakeholders?
f. How frequently is this item or protocol adapted to meet the context?

2. Participants ask clarifying and probing questions to better find evidence of whiteness or antidotes to whiteness in either the item or protocol, the process by which the item or protocol was created, or how the item or protocol is used.

3. Participants share findings.

    a. Where was whiteness present?
    b. Where were antidotes successfully implemented?
    c. What was unclear?

4. Participants make recommendations to challenge areas of whiteness that were found, utilizing the note-capturing s in Table 3.1.

When white folx start to admit to the racist legacy that has shaped our daily experiences, we frequently rely on the people of color in our lives to show us another way. We bring books by authors of color into our white classrooms, we hang posters of famous Black folx in our white spaces, and we partially adopt the works of Gholdy Muhammad, Chris Emdin, Cornelius Minor, Gloria Ladson-Billings, and so many other Black and brown pedagogical geniuses. Often, we do these things without first weeding out whiteness, and so risk developing racially tolerant children who will continue to cause harm. To protest whiteness, to reimagine what whiteness has created, and to do teaching, learning, and

TABLE 3.1 Note-Capturing Tool

White Norm(s)	Evidence of Whiteness	Evidence of Antidote to Whiteness
Perfectionism Sense of Urgency Quantity Over Quality Worship of the Written Word Only One Right Way Paternalism Either/Or Thinking Power Hoarding Individualism Progress is Bigger/More Objectivity		

schooling differently is not a small ask. In majority white spaces, it is even more challenging to do this work in a way that does not cause harm to any students of color in those learning spaces. It is not the burden of students of color to teach their white peers other ways of doing and being, nor do they need to engage in the same sort of decentering work. Students of color should be encouraged to celebrate and share their cultures and should be invited to be active participants in creating classroom agreements but should not feel obligated to reimagine a way of doing and being that was never theirs to begin with. In such cases as these, teachers must support students to recognize that whiteness has shaped how we all move in the world, but also that only white people have enough power in this country to have the privilege that allows us to protest through sacrifice. As Baldwin explains,

> the crucial paradox which confronts us here is that the whole process of education occurs within a social framework and is designed to perpetuate the aims of society.... What societies really, ideally, want is a citizenry which will simply obey the rules of society. If a society succeeds in this, that society is about to perish. The obligation of anyone who thinks of himself as responsible is to examine

society and try to change it and to fight it – at no matter what risk. This is the only hope society has. This is the only way societies change.[20]

So, for white folx, the ultimate protest is sacrifice. To sacrifice the comfort of the society we know. To give up whiteness. Being an antiracist, emerging abolitionist, and white educator who is committed to a pedagogy of protest—*pedagogical parrhesia*—means recognizing, with boldness and frankness and self-criticality, that our way of doing and being carries a legacy of causing harm to Black, brown, and Indigenous folx.

Notes

1. Margaret A. Hagerman. (2018). *White Kids: Growing Up with Privilege in a Racially Divided America*. New York: NYU Press, 206.
2. Hagerman, 208.
3. Gillian B. White. (2015, September 30). *The Troubling Link Between School Funding and Race*. The Atlantic. Retrieved from: https://www.theatlantic.com/business/archive/2015/09/public-school-funding-and-the-role-of-race/408085/
4. M. Wilbur. (2021, January 19). *Form Based Code to Impact Chappaqua's Enrollment | The Examiner News*. The Examiner News | SMALL NEWS IS BIG NEWS. Retrieved from: https://www.theexaminernews.com/form-based-code-would-produce-modestly-higher-enrollment-hike-in-chappaqua-schools/
5. M. Wilbur. (2020, November 3). *Opposition Stiffens to New Castle Form Based Code at Hearing | The Examiner News*. The Examiner News | SMALL NEWS IS BIG NEWS. Retrieved from: https://www.theexaminernews.com/opposition-stiffens-to-new-castle-form-based-code-at-hearing/
6. Where the Best Public High Schools Are Located. (n.d.). Retrieved from:https://www.usnews.com/education/besthigh-schools/articles/where-the-best-public-high-schools-are-located
7. Hagerman, 209.

8. B. Walsh, D. DaGradi, R. Stevenson, J. Andrews, D. D. Van, D. Tomlinson, G. Johns et al. (1964). *Mary Poppins*. Burbank, CA: Distributed by Walt Disney Studios Home Entertainment.
9. Bettina Love. (2020). "There is nothing fragile about racism." Retrieved on December 9, 2020 from: https://www.edweek.org/leadership/opinion-there-is-nothing-fragile-about-racism/2020/08
10. Joyce E. King. (1991). "Dysconscious Racism: Ideology, Identity, and the Miseducation of Teachers." *The Journal of Negro Education*, vol. 60, no. 2: 133–146.
11. James Baldwin. (1998). "The White Man's Guilt." *Collected Essays*. New York: Penguin Putnam, 723.
12. Kenneth Jones and Tema Okun (2001). "White Supremacy Culture." *Dismantling Racism: A Workbook for Social Change Groups*. Changework. Retrieved from: https://www.thc.texas.gov/public/upload/preserve/museums/files/White_Supremacy_Culture.pdf
13. Joyce E. King. (1991). "Dysconscious Racism: Ideology, Identity, and the Miseducation of Teachers." *The Journal of Negro Education*, vol. 60, no. 2: 135.
14. James Baldwin. (1984). "On Being White and Other Lies." Originally published in *Essence*, 90–92.
15. bell hooks. (2015). *Black Looks: Race and Representation*. New York: Routledge.
16. Alice Walker. (1981). "The Dummy in the Window: Joel Chandler Harris and the Invention of Uncle Remus." From *Living by the World: Selected Writings 1973–1987*. San Diego: Harcourt Brace Jovanovich.
17. Toni Morrison. (1993). *Playing in the Dark: Whiteness and the Literary Imagination*. New York: Vintage Books.
18. Stokely Carmichael and Charles V. Hamilton. (1992). *Black Power: The Politics of Liberation in America*. New York: Random House.
19. Claudia Rankine. (2020). *Just Us: An American Conversation*. Minneapolis, Minnesota: Graywolf Press.
20. James Baldwin. (1963). A Talk to Teachers. Originally published in *The Saturday Review*. Retrieved from: https://richgibson.com/talktoteachers.htm

4

But If Faced With Courage: Talk About History in Today's Context

Protest-in-Context

As William ("Bill") Jefferson Clinton took the oath of office for the highest office in American democracy, the presidency, on January 21, 1993, the thematic refrain was one of sacrifice and individual responsibility in service to the communality of this nation. "There is nothing wrong with America that cannot be cured by what is right with America." After his inaugural address, writer, poet, and civil rights activity, Maya Angelou, born in 1928, recited a poem "On the Pulse of Morning," which poignantly shared the thematic overtone of Clinton's appeal for hopeful change and collective responsibility. Grounding her inimitably humane appeal in history—a core approach to parrhesia, critical to a radically human imagination—Angelou called upon the American consciousness to reconcile the meaningful arc between our nation's abhorrent yesterday and its yet-to-be-defined tomorrow.[1] To hear the poem's metaphoric imagery, conversational passion, and deeply maternal rhythm in her own

DOI: 10.4324/9781003183365-4

voice, you can watch a YouTube video of Angelou reading the poem aloud at Clinton's inauguration by using a smartphone to scan the accompanying QR code.

At the heart of Angelou's proposition about history is courage. Courage to know and situate ourselves in the historical narrative of this nation, refusing to prevaricate and/or revise the vilest chapters, characters, and content for the comfort of the oppressors nor for the soothing of the oppressed. Courage to face, without dread, the enduring isms and phobias that perpetuate a national binary of what Karl Marx identified as the bourgeoisie and the proletariat, and what we colloquially categorize as the haves and have nots. Courage to maintain a sense of moral consciousness, which preserves our capacity, first, and then our willingness to see in the quotidian affairs of today's world, echoes, waves, and shadows of the wrenching pains of yesterday. As pedagogical protestors, utilizing our classrooms to emancipate the being and thinking and doing of our students, it is our responsibility to ensure that when we approach the instruction of history, *all history*, we do so "faced with courage." When faced with courage, we both refute the diluting of history and we negate any faux proposition that the oppressive thoughts and tactics of whiteness expired with a generation before us.

Of all the content areas at risk of capitulating to the specter of revisionist isolationism, history is unmatched. Beyond the unsurprising pedagogical challenges of limited historical knowledge about particular eras and movements, implicit—and explicit—national, social, cultural, political, and/or religious biases, and a lack of meaningful correlations between content areas, many educators are challenged by—which assumes they make an effort in the first place—the task of bridging historical knowledge to today's context. If, in fact, history is as Mamta Aggarwal describes, "the drama of the human beings on the stage of the world which is still growing on,"[2] then history in isolation of today's context disservices history of its pedagogical production. As American educators, when we teach content that is grounded in national history—chattel slavery, the Declaration of Independence, exploitation of Indigenous Americans, the Civil War, Women's Suffrage, the stock market crash of 1929 and subsequent Great Depression, Franklin Delano Roosevelt and the New Deal, the bombing of Hiroshima and Nagasaki Jim Crow and the Civil Rights Movement, the queer riots of Stonewall, the terrorist attacks of September 11, 2001, and even the election of Donald J. Trump and the state-sanctioned resurgence of white supremacist violence by self-deputized citizens—we are often trained to approach these defining markers without bridging the arc into today's context. Yet, historical narratives realize their meaningfulness and consequential effect when intentionally and intimately framed in ways that form and inform how individuals, structures, and societies are interwoven into a present-day network of democratic possibility.

Classrooms are among the critical sociocultural and sociopolitical institutions responsible for ensuring the sustainability and meaning-making of national narratives about the past; and synchronously. They can function as sites of pedagogical protest as easily as they can embody the posterities of past inequities. They are either sites of pedagogical parrhesia against the inequities of history or sites of sustained inequity. Either we are teaching history, faced with courage, to demonstrate how to deconstruct and dismantle "its wrenching pain" in today's world; or we are teaching history, faced with cowardice, to merely pardon ourselves from the bloodied rot of national antiquity. Against the backdrop of standardization and packaged curricula, one might inquire: who decides if we teach history with today's context in mind, bridging what has occurred with what's occurring? The distinct answer for pedagogical parrhesia is: *you do*. If our shared pursuit is the emancipation of all folx—again, *all means all*—then how we approach national narratives about the past will determine if we are using our classrooms to cultivate more engaged, responsible, democratic citizens who know that, "if faced with courage," the history they are learning "need not be lived again." When our classrooms and schools are situated in communities—rural, suburban, and urban—where racial and ethnic divisions, structural and generational poverty, political mistrust, food and healthcare apartheids, and hyperviolent policing remain endemic, how students think about history shapes their sense of democratic hope and communal consciousness about a future where justice and freedom alleviate those indicators of human suffering.

Any discourse around the teaching of history, particularly within American classrooms, needs to first acknowledge that classrooms are politically charged, value-laden sites of competing narratives, lived experiences and knowledge, intentional—and unintentional—silences, and, miserably, employability compliance. In sum, teaching history is not an agnostic practice, and yet, to maintain employment, so many are expected to approach it as such. Thus, the proposition of teaching history within the context of today's world unavoidably presumes that folx committed to pedagogical parrhesia vehemently reject the normativity of political and ethical agnosticism that habitually infiltrates history-focused pedagogy. Teachers of history who are also pedagogical parrhesiastic educators must understand that history is only a discipline but also a mechanism of power. The primary goal, then, of history within the classroom is to cultivate a context for engagement—faced with courage—whereby students make sense, make meaning, and make connections between past affairs and present complexities.

One of the challenges within this approach is that educators, particularly white folx, were themselves raised within educational and mass media systems that actively perpetuated ahistorical teachings. An additional challenge is that educators will have to submit to a non-linear historical narrative, and, potentially, a narrative that both assumes and salutes disjointed chronology. Still another challenge is that educators will have to be sensitive to the social-emotional hardships experienced by students engaging with vile and traumatizing moments in our national historical narrative, while they concurrently grapple with contemporary assaults against vulnerable people—Black, brown, queer, and beyond. In a cultural moment exhausted by oppression-anxiety, we as educators cannot always know of the psychological precarities of our students and their families, for whom the arc of wrenching pain between yesterday and today can be triggering. Yet the very premise of pedagogical parrhesia—speaking truth to the powers of individuals, structures, and systems—demands a critical, radically human(e) open discourse.

Most of our students, particularly Black and brown students, pragmatically expect a clear and compelling rationale for *why* something historical will be meaningful to their education before it can be learned, analyzed, and internalized. Our responsibility, then, is to provide that why for students—a why that is grounded in knowing that history is not only an insight into what has been but also a catalyst for protesting what is and reimagining what can be. History, in this framing, becomes of function of "prophetic, tactful pedagogy," which, in part, is a "penetrating criticism that allows one to *see* possibilities that are otherwise hidden by the actual conditions present in a given situation."[3] By imagining beyond the knowledge of history or the assumed facts of historical narratives, situating the present as a poetic function of what was once conceived of as an impossibility, and using that to model what we have to conceive, we can offer students an accessibility to history that transcends the isolated, risky revisionism so many educators are complicit with.

What is pedagogically parrhesiastic about esteeming Frederick McKinley Jones' refrigerated-truck ingenuity *without* discussing Trump-era cuts to the Supplemental

Nutrition Assistance Program (SNAP), effectively sustaining food apartheids—areas structurally without easy access to fresh and nutritious foods—in lower-income urban and rural communities? What is pedagogically parrhesiastic to know of the first successful pericardium surgery performed by Dr. Daniel Hale Williams *without* talk of persistent healthcare disparities between Black folx, Latinx folx, and white folx, and the biases of medical practitioners who disregard the symptoms of Black women, particularly during maternity? What is pedagogically parrhesiastic about being moved by the words of the Reverend Dr. Martin Luther King Jr.'s nonviolent protests and the Civil Rights Era of the 1950s and 1960s *without* talk of today's hyperviolent policing tactics and Draconian curfews against Black Lives Matter movements?

I recall teaching a fifth-grade class, in 2011, where I introduced Garrett Morgan's three-light traffic-signal system. Of all the Black inventors, Morgan has unceasingly captivated my imagination. Like countless Black students in the early twentieth century, he was forced into labor to alleviate the financial scarcities of his family, thus "quitting" school—as many biographical précises of his life tend to label his educational verdict. Leaning into a spirit of resilience, Morgan ultimately continued his academic pursuits by using a portion of his income to employ a private tutor. Eventually, Morgan invented products ranging from hair-straightening cream to a safety smoke hood to a traffic control device.

On a rather uneventful Monday, one of my most rambunctious, immensely thoughtful, and deeply sensitive students, Kevin—a Black, male, only child, who perpetually sought a persuasive *why* within his learning process—blurted, "Mr. Harvey, who cares? That was like a hundred years ago, right? Isn't he dead?"

Recalling that Kevin and his family lived in one of the more congested, economically vulnerable, and underinvested sections of Boston, I immediately replied, "Do you like sitting in traffic, Kevin?"

"No!" he dramatically shouted, embodying the hopeful performer he aspired to be in the future.

I replied to the class. "Show of hands: who wants to be in a car accident when you leave school?" Was it the most trauma-sensitive question? No. Would I change the framing of it if I were still in the classroom? Highly likely. Most students laughed, of course, and consecutively offered a melody of—

"No!"

"I don't!"

"Nobody likes accidents!"

"And neither do I!" I went on.

> Now, I want you to imagine how many accidents there would be and how much traffic we'd have if not for the inventiveness of Garrett Morgan and his three-light traffic device *with* a warning signal. Could you imagine only having a two-light system of 'go' and 'stop'?

Ashlee, an infrequently vocal student, raised her hand. When I called on her, she said,

> No, I can't imagine that. We need the yellow light because it not only tells cars to slow down, but it tells people walking and riding bikes that they only have a few seconds to get across the street. He ... he kind of, like, saved the lives of walkers and bike-riders, too.

Amya was itching to engage.

> Who determines how many traffic lights a city or a neighborhood gets, Mr. Harvey? Is it based on the number

of streets in the area, or the amount of people who live there, or, like, the number of cars, or is it something else?

I replied,

> Ah! Brilliant question. We are talking about a *traffic* light system, which ensures that automobiles, along with pedestrians and bikers, as Ashlee mentioned, are *transported* safely to their destinations. What department within a city might be responsible for managing *traffic* lights? Think about the two words I've stressed: traffic and transported.

The answers poured in—

> "Uh ... the department of traffic?"
> "No! It's the department of DMV ... my mom hates the DMV."
> "The DMV is the department of vehicles."
> "It's the DMV, right, Mr. Harvey? They manage all the vehicles." Ashlee raised her hand, again. "Mmm, the department of transportation."
> "Exactly, Ashlee—thank you! Amya, what department is responsible for the traffic light system in a city?"
> "The department of transportation," she replied.
> The class repeated, in unison, "The department of transportation."
> "What kind of factors might the department of transportation use to determine the number and location of traffic lights in a city?" I inquired, assuming I would hold the burden of the cognitive lift. I assumed imperfectly. The answers poured in—
> "Number of accidents."
> "Maybe they match them to bus routes."
> "In places where people walk a lot, like parks."
> "Where schools are ... or where lots of old people live."

Ashlee shifted the tone and tenor of the responses when she answered, "Where rich people live."

"Would you like to explain?" I asked, longing that she would. (And also, that she would recall that our class had normed the use of terms like *higher-income neighborhoods* or *higher-income communities* instead of "rich people.")

Warily, but resolutely, she did.

> When we are in higher-income neighborhoods with lots of big houses, driveways, parks, and things like that, they have really beautiful traffic lights. I don't know if they have more, but they are different than the ones in our neighborhood. Ours are on those regular silver poles. In the rich ... I mean, higher-income neighborhoods, their poles have pillars of brick with sayings. And their street names light-up on both sides ... there's a light in their street name boxes.

"Would anyone like to respond to, build on, or disagree with what Ashlee shared?"

Malachi spoke up. "Do *those* neighborhoods have more or less traffic lights than *we* do?"

Tragically, a symptom of white supremacy, invoking them-us dichotomies was conventional framing for social and cultural phenomena. I replied, "What do you think, Malachi? Think about what you've seen in various neighborhoods you've visited or driven through. Where did you see more traffic signals, and where did you see less of them?"

A handful of students responded—

"They have less!"
"You can drive for days without having to stop in some neighborhoods!"

Karon shared, "I think they have less, because the neighborhoods are more spread out."

> Think about what Karon just offered us. He believes that higher-income neighborhoods have less traffic signals

because the neighborhood is more spread out, which in transportation terms we'd call, "low-density." I'm going to put that word on the board, and I want you to write it down, because we will come back to that soon. You should know that low-density communities have less residents, therefore less traffic, therefore less traffic jams, and therefore less traffic signals. Do you see how that works?

"Yes!" Malachi reacted avidly. He then had a parrhesiastic notion, for a fifth grader, about low-density zoning and its inferences about race and economics. "So, lower-income neighborhoods *need* more traffic signals because more people live in them. So why doesn't the department of whatever just spread the people out from the lower-income neighborhoods into neighborhoods where there is more space?"

Bridging the moral act of history from yesterday to today allowed us—a community of beautifully brilliant Black and brown young people—to make meaningful connections between what inspired Morgan to design his signal in 1922 and how traffic signals have become sociocultural and socioeconomic indicators of place and place-based privilege. What began as a lesson about historical engineering at the turn of the century morphed into pedagogical parrhesia.

Protest-in-Practice

Teachers must understand the historical origins of the math we study, the science we take as fact, and the literature we value. Several years ago, while I was working with teaching residents to determine texts worthy of being taught in our classes, a heated debate began about whether we should use compelling books taught by authors with controversial personal or political lives. Several of the residents felt strongly that authors like Roald Dahl, Dr. Seuss, and Charles Dickens did not belong in an abolitionist classroom while others thought the works should be judged separate from the persons who created the works. Through this debate, we began considering how we can study individual works while paying close attention to the context in which they were created. In fact, we realized that the context shaped the texts and so was integral to the teaching of the texts. If the text is a necessary part of the curriculum, we must ask ourselves how we might present materials within the context they were created. To do this, we must know *our* history.

When working with aspiring teachers, one of the first things we do together is to study the history of oppression and racism in this country. We find the threads of current oppression throughout our history and connect modern day racism to the founding of our country. Once, in a class, when I defined racism as being rooted in historical power, a student argued that he did not see the purpose of including history within the definition. He asked, "isn't understanding who has power *now* enough?" The most obvious answer for an educator committed to pedagogical parrhesia is no. If we attempt to interrupt modern day oppression without understanding all of the nuanced ways it is woven into the fabric of our society—markers of history, but not restricted to history—we will never be able to fully eradicate it.

Pedagogical parrhesia demands that we connect the past to the present and plan for a better future; if educators cannot find the racism in a moment in United States history or how it shapes our lived experiences, they are missing a piece of the puzzle. Everything in our history is a product of, or a response to, racism. Teachers who believe teaching is an act of protest feel successful only when their students use history as a tool to demand change. As a student at Clemson University, A.D. Carson modeled the power of connecting our past to our present when he created his lyrical call to action, *See the Stripes*:

> *The site of "the most exciting 25 seconds in college football"*
> *was made possible by profits from the most shameful centuries in*
> *America's history.*
>
> *Those are the stripes we bear,*
> *and before you decide to wear*
> *that orange tee, or that painted paw,*
> *think,*
> *for a moment, about those stripes,*
> *think*
> *of the backs of the slaves,*
> *think*
> *about the strips of land,*
> *and the sharecroppers tied to it after so-called emancipation,*
> *think*
> *of the uniform of that 13 year old boy,*
> *a slave of the state,*
> *forced to help build the first buildings at this place,*
> *think*
> *of the dark matters that matter more than you know—*
> *the difference between willing ignorance and active participation,*
> *complicit denial and abject perpetuation—*
>
> *before you*
> *think*
> *"Solid Orange,"*
> *think*
> *of how ridiculous a Solid Orange Tiger would look.*
> *Think*
> *of seeing its stripes,*
> *think*
> *of* being *its stripes,*

*and think
of how terrible it is
to not be seen,
to not be acknowledged,*

*think
about never being doomed to repeat
an atrocious history,
and being better*

*because of knowing better
and doing better
because as things are now,
we are The Tigers,
built on a legacy of slavery, sharecropping and convict labor,
by slave owners, supremacists and segregationists,*

*but come to the campus of Clemson University,
and you'd hardly be able to tell it from looking around.*[4]

Too often, educators do not take the time to follow the threads of history into today's lived experiences. In the teacher preparation program in which I work, the very first course, which every teacher candidate takes, requires students to study the history of race and racism in our schools. In one assignment, we attempt to unweave the fabric of today's educational system by tracing the roots of racism, one educational practice at a time. For example, a student might choose to learn more about why we have so many racially segregated schools in our state. In order to fully understand this trend, that student would most likely study the racist roots of the Federal Housing Administration, racial steering, blockbusting, redlining, exclusionary zoning, property tax laws, movements to decentralize school systems, charter and voucher systems, racial covenants, white flight, and so much more. In this assignment, aspiring teachers are expected to scrutinize one aspect of our system, but the hope is that they will soon discover that, because so much of American history is built on racism, when we are approaching any historically rooted lesson, the question we must always ask ourselves—during internalization, planning, and instruction—is, "How is this racist and how does it affect our lives today?"

A Guiding Questions Approach

In addition to this foundational question, here is a set of ten guiding questions to ask and answer in your planning and preparation when researching a historically situated topic, which will effectively generate inquiry-based pedagogy:

1. Where is there evidence of this event/moment/person in today's world (laws/policies/demographics/culture/language)?
2. What are the ripple effects that this event/moment/person caused in the coming years, decades, and centuries?
3. What precedents were set by this event/moment/person?
4. How was the world at that moment the same or different from today? On the other hand, how is today's world similar to the world of the past? Use specific cultural, social, and political indicators.
5. Who were the people involved with this event/moment/person and how can we relate to those folx?
6. Where are their indicators of reimagined oppression within this current event? Is the current oppressor connected to whomever has historically been the oppressor?
7. Who and how were young people responsible for engaging and/or leading around [x] event/moment/person in history, as a point of entry for today's young people?
8. Where do we see artists, writers, and cultural architects engaging historical moments and concepts in today's world, offering new interpretations and connections?

9. What social-emotional sensitivities demand intentionality and unpacking as we unpack this event/moment/movement/person in today's context?
10. *For our math folx*—what about this word problem, or the names used, or the context framed is situated in a larger historical context that is requisite background knowledge for understanding the problem?

As a practice of pedagogical parrhesia, particularly the values of frankness and duty, you must be prepared to wrestle with how asking and answering the aforementioned questions will help you develop guiding questions with students. The provided guided questions are mostly situated in four categories: **causal**—"what," **explanatory**—"why," **evaluative**—"how," and **socio-locational**—"where." Notice that none of the questions start with "should" or "could," because pedagogical protest with young people avoids inferring a non-critical judgment. Instead, inquiry-based pedagogical protest is about guiding young people to do the cognitive heavy-lifting of making connections between yesterday and today through a series of questions that intentionally opens each sepal,[5] revealing a parrhesiastic encounter.

A Culture of Skepticism

Beyond educating themselves to be critical consumers of today's content through a historical lens and history's content through today's lens, teachers should create a culture of skepticism within their classrooms—a kind of skepticism of today's events/moments/movements grounded in yesterday's *frank* realities. Our country was founded on skepticism by skeptics. To be a skeptic is to be a seeker, and within pedagogical parrhesia, it is to be a seeker out of a sense of moral duty. In classrooms across this country, we celebrate artists, writers, poets, politicians, and philosophers who questioned moral authority and challenged the espoused "truths" of institutional establishments—both of which are forms of protest. From John Locke's political theories of the rights of the governed to Emerson's claim in his essay *Politics*, "Every actual State is corrupt. Good men must not obey the laws too well,"[6] we tell our young people that protest is the foundation of what makes this country a distinctive democracy.

Yet, we do not value that same level of skepticism and protest in all of our historical figures. We let Locke, Emerson, Thoreau, Tolstoy, William James, and so many more white men stand as forefathers of American protest thought while we imprison, murder, villainize, or forget figures like Reverend George Lee, Marcus Garvey, Mae Mallory, Huey P. Newton, Tecumseh, Malcolm X, and other Black and brown skeptics and pedagogical parrhesiastics who changed the course of history in this country. We often fall short in teaching our young people to revolt in the ways the white men did who are honored by this nation, but all of these men learned to be skeptics and so can all of our students. The most effective teachers not only teach the history of these great protestors, but they teach the art of skepticism as the foundation of protest. Before young people can "speak truth to power," they must learn to be skeptical of power.

At the start of a unique school year during the COVID-19 pandemic, my husband was gearing up to teach his students virtually. During the first week of school, I sat on the couch in his office and watched him greet his classes. Instead of using those first days, as he usually would, to practice the systems and routines that allow students to share physical space, he jumped right into the routines that would allow them to share intellectual space. He told them they would design "a classroom culture for historians and activists; people who use the past to change the future." He told them they would learn through questioning, through contextualizing facts, and through connecting what they know to what they discover in this class. From there, he turned on song by Taylor Swift about how all men cheat on their girlfriends. He asked, "What shapes her opinion?" As students shared rumors about the breakup that led to that song, he asked a series of questions, including:

1. How does that shape her opinion?
2. What facts is she sharing?
3. How do you know those are facts?
4. How are her experiences shaping her perception of the world?
5. What is the emotional tone here? What language did she use to tell you that?
6. How is her platform helping her shape this story?
7. What don't we know?
8. Whose voice isn't helping tell this story and set this tone?

Over the coming weeks, as I floated in and out of his office, I watched him use these same questions, whether he was working with students to explore opinion pieces, textbooks, laws, or historical documents. One day in early October, as his senior class was beginning to read about the articles of the Constitution, I walked in just in time to hear a student ask, "What does the author mean by "supremacy of the people?" Which people does he think the constitution makes supreme? How does he know?" Through my husband's careful modeling of skeptical thinking, this student had learned to question her sources and challenge what she was being told as fact. She had learned to pedagogically inquire for "the other side of the story," a seemingly simple tool that many, if not all of us, were told at some point during our adolescent upbringings. He built her up to this moment in the following ways:

1. Start with material—song lyrics, visual art, a movie, a familiar story—that is easily accessible to all students; something that is culturally relevant and part of their

daily lives. As students make meaning of the piece, ask them to consider:

   a. What facts and opinions are shared?
   b. What influences what the creator decides to share and omit?
   c. How the creator's life influences their creation?
   d. What the emotional tone is (through imagery, word choice, structure, etc.)?
   e. How the time and place influenced the creation?

2. Move to materials that are clearly rooted in opinion or emotion but may not already be familiar to young people. As the material is analyzed and internalized, ask them what they need to find out, know more about, or better understand in order to answer the above questions. Support them in framing a list of unknowns. For example, as students look at a poem written by James Baldwin, along with the above questions, they might add:

   a. When and where did he live?
   b. What was going on in his place and space that may have influences his thinking?
   c. What were his identities?
   d. How did his identities affect the way he moved through the world?
   e. Who influenced his thinking?
   f. What did he value and why?
   g. Who else was writing at that time and how is their perspective different? On the other hand, how is their perspective aligned?

3. At this time, take a step back to define *objectivity* and *subjectivity* with students:

   a. Use some of the exploration you have already done and extend their thinking by looking at primary

sources about the same issue from two different perspectives. Obituaries of a controversial historical figure or opinion pieces about a political issue might work.
   b. Compare the message and tone of each piece using the above questioning techniques.
   c. Ask them what in the obituaries is fact and what is interpretation of the facts. Skeptical students will recognize that facts are interpreted by the people who convey them and so are always corrupted by subjectivity.
4. Once students have done this foundational work, encourage them to use this line of questioning while exploring all historically situated topics. Ideally, the students will no longer offer their research, writings, and presentations as fact, but rather as well-reasoned, well-supported arguments.

This type of learning is most meaningful when students' access points are connected to their personal contexts. Students often struggle to identify areas for probing when there is obscurity in locating the human aspects of the content they are learning, the issues that endure across place and space—desire for freedom, for power, for sustenance. So, teachers who hope to develop young skeptics always ask students, "What does this remind you of in your life and how does that help you better understand what is going on here?" Connecting the content to what we know can help us consider what we have yet to discover.

Notes

1. Maya Angelou. (1993). *The Inaugural Poem: On the Pulse of Morning.* New York: Random House.
2. Mamta Aggarwal. (2017). "Six Problems Faced by History Teachers in Teaching History." *History Discussion.* Retrieved from: https://www.historydiscussion.net/teaching/6-problems-faced-by-history-teacher-in-teaching-history/495

3. Mark D. Vagle. (2008). "Searching for a Prophetic Tactful Pedagogy: An Attempt to Deepen the Knowledge, Skills, and Dispositions Discourse around Good Teaching." *E&C/Education and Culture*, vol. 24, no. 1: 155.
4. Carson, A.D. (2017). See the Stripes [Recorded by A.D. Carson]. On *Owning My Masters* [Digital Album]. Clemson, South Carolina: Soundcloud.
5. When a flower is a bud, it is surrounded by sepals, which in many cases are green, as in this example. They protect the flower bud and are behind/underneath the petals when the flower opens.
6. Ralph Waldo Emerson. (1983). *Ralph Waldo Emerson Essays and Lectures*. New York: Library of America.

5

Two Sides of the Same Coin: Talk About Power, Not Only Oppression

Protest-in-Context

When 24-year-old organizer Stokely Carmichael ascended the stage of the Greek Theater at the University of California at Berkeley on Saturday, October 29, 1966, more than 10,000 people inundated the open-air amphitheater zoned for only 8,500. As the rhetorical provocateur for a conference planned and sponsored by the *Students for a Democratic Society*—a national student organization with an anti-war, free-speech platform—Carmichael was preparing to speak to a largely white aggregation assembled with a publicized intent to raise money for the Student Nonviolence Coordinating Committee (SNCC), of which he was at the helm. Adding to the production value of his primary proposition, he spoke from behind a podium with a skimpily constructed sign reading, "Black Power and its Challenges."

Following his arrest for protesting in the March Against Fear in Greenwood, Mississippi, which had occurred five months earlier, Carmichael dissented the nonviolent approach. "We've

DOI: 10.4324/9781003183365-5

been saying 'Freedom' for six years," referencing the philosophy of nonviolence espoused by the National Association for the Advancement of Colored People (NAACP), Congress for Racial Equality (CORE), Southern Christian Leadership Conference (SCLC), Martin Luther King, Jr., John Lewis, James Bevel, and countless civil rights leaders in the South. "What we are going to start saying now is Black Power." Civil rights organizers in the generation preceding Carmichael saw and heard "Back Powers" as a militant clarion call for race wars between Black and white folx. Carmichael was pressed to abandon the phrase, and the confrontational approach, but he refused and amplified the call. During this first stop at Berkeley on a two-year tour of college campuses, opining haunting elocutions with intentional effort to agitate "an audience of middle-class whites,"[1] he realized that intention. The ardor of this gathering was intensified against the backdrop of the California gubernatorial election in which Ronald Reagan, a Republican and later the 40th president of the United States, attempted to politically weaponize Carmichael's invitation to and participation in the conference for his own gain with the very white, middle-class folx Carmichael rhetorically condemned.

In this 53 minute treatise, Carmichael introduced the premise and invoked the use of the word "power" 19 times, attempting to get Black and white folx "to explore their positions in relation to each other and to the power structures of society."[2]

> We won't get caught up in questions about power. This country knows what power is. It knows what Black Power is because it deprived black people of it for over four hundred years. White people associate Black Power with violence because of their own inability to deal with blackness. If we had said "Negro power" nobody would get scared. Everybody would support it. If we said power for colored people, everybody'd be for that, but it is the word "black" that bothers people in this country, and

that's their problem, not mine. That's the lie that says anything black is bad.[3]

From his vantage point, folx committed to the emancipation of Black folx needed to accept the role of power in white folx's limited views on emancipation—how it is realized and who has access to it. At a moment in the racial advancement of parrhesia, as Black folx were "speaking truth to power" at all levels of influence, Carmichael revolutionarily compelled protestors and civil rights organizers to situate their claims of oppression and injustice within a rhetorical and political framework that necessitated white folx to internally and outwardly confront their proximity to, maintenance of, and complicity with *power*.

For our pedagogical purposes, power is defined as structural access to and use of control over systems, resources, and individuals. A pedagogical exploration of power compels all of us to situate ourselves relative to the systems and resources which either power over us, or through which we are in power. As a reflective and reflexive discourse, power distinctively invites two kinds of experiential truths—structural and relational. Ironically, however, the oft-used paradox of structural and relational are not only interconnected, but also mutually dependent in all facets of democratic society, including in schools and classrooms. Yet, there has been a noticeable lack of pedagogical attention to, engagement with, and instruction about *power* as a sociopolitical and sociocultural mechanism in current dialogues about freedom, equity, and justice. In its place, there is a pathological fixation with discussions about oppression and inequity, which are the deficit side of power; nevertheless, two sides of the same coin. For Carmichael, it was not only politically critical but human(e)ly necessary to controvert discussions about *freedom* with *power*, as a rhetorically revolutionary tool to unambiguously interrogate white—and even some Black—assumptions that freedom might be attained without a deconstruction and redistribution of power. Likewise, in classrooms committed to pedagogical parrhesia, we must deliberately utilize our teaching and learning to guide our students in interrogating power as the underside of oppression.

"You know what I'm sick of, now that white people want to talk about racism and injustice, all of a sudden?" a Black educator, Mrs. Barbara, probed rhetorically. Now in her 26th year in the classroom, Mrs. Barbara—or "Mrs. B-Good" according to her Zoom name—was attending a webinar centered on how educators of diverse races can support each other in confronting questions of race in the classroom.

> White people, especially white women, wanting to talk about oppression and pain, injustice and struggle, what's not fair and what's not right. And you know why? Because that's the feel-good conversation. I want to talk about power. Because that's the political conversation, and our kids, especially Black and Latino kids, need to hear about how power works so they don't think all of this injustice and oppression is a result of hocus pocus.

Sheepishly, a white teacher, Alison, who was relatively new the classroom compared to most folx in the webinar, replied,

> Do kids really need to learn about power? It feels like an adult conversation, not really a child conversation. We don't want to alarm *them* too early about the world ... or put *our* stuff on *them*. You know, adult stuff.

Mrs. Barbara pushed back.

> Do our students experience the effects and traumas of power? Do the Black and Latino students in your classroom more than likely realize that you have more power than their mothers and grandmothers and aunties and them because of the color of *your* skin? Do *you* realize

you have more power because of the color of your skin? The last time I checked, as a middle-aged Black mother of Black boys, it is *never too early* to talk about *your* stuff. You know, *white* stuff. When I think about the ways this nation will not-so-gently remind my sons about their reduced power compared to the white folx they encounter, I don't have a choice but to talk about power.

"I am so sorry, I didn't mean to offend you. That's not how I mean it," Alison responded, seemingly defeated, holding her hands flat and tightly to the chest.

Power claims that it never means to offend, but offense is its nourishment. And that's why we need to talk about it, because Black children are regularly offended by white folx and your power. If we ... if I never use *my* classroom to teach the babies who look like *me* about power and how it works in this country, I risk sending them into *your* world not knowing what to do when they're *offended*.

Alison replied clumsily, still attempting to refine and reiterate her point while most of the Black and brown folx on the webinar turned our cameras off to hide our embarrassment for Alison.

That is so real, and I agree with all of that, Mrs. Barbara. I just don't want us to spend so much time talking about power and oppression that we forget to give *them* hope. Isn't that what all of us need? Hope that the oppression and power we're enduring now will end in this generation.

Frustratedly and brazenly, Mrs. Barbara offered her final word.

I'm going to say this and be done with it. If the power of white folx and its oppression over the rest of us was resolved by hope, then we wouldn't have endured plantation slavey, Jim Crow, the myth of the welfare queen, or the killing of Black people in broad daylight. Period. Hope has its place, but hope is *not* enough when you are the ones without power, without privilege, without rights, without freedom. I know that's hard for you to comprehend because you have never lived without any of those, but I have lived my entire life without them in this nation. And my mother lived her entire life without it. And her mother the same. And now, my boys are living without it. So, no, hope is not what all of us need. What *all* of us need is for *all* of us to get clear and to be honest about where we stand in our relationship to power.

Mrs. Barbara reinforced a Stokely-esque ethic with her pedagogically parrhesiastic remark, "Hope has its place, but hope is not enough when you are the ones without power." According to Stokely, the nonviolent movement's talk of freedom was a moral discussion, while his talk of power was a political one. "We have been unable to grasp it [political awareness] because we've always been moving in the field of morality and love while people have been politically jiving with our lives."[4] In American classrooms, far too often, the preoccupation with talking about oppression is a type of privileging of an individual morality and a placid, can-we-all-just-get-along discussion, while the avoidance of talking about power is an underprivileging of a structural one. But any structural discussion about power, in classrooms full of Black and brown young people, must not be void of naming the premise that access to, maintenance of, and complicity with power is based on "whites being systemically privileged in our society, whether or not white people are actively conscious of and/or pursuing such privilege."[5] If they are to understand how dismantling and redistributing power facilitates emancipation for all folx, students must be engaged with the ways in which personal, interpersonal, cultural, and institutional privilege occurs for and advantages white folx at the expense of marginalized identities in this nation. Moreover, by centering how social identities beyond race—physical ability (able-bodied), sexuality (heterosexual), gender (male), religion (Christian), socioeconomic (middle-class and higher-earning), language (English-speaking)—are privileged, students are invited to analyze *their* proximity to power and privilege. Any engagement with power and privilege in our pedagogical parrhesia requires an intentionally external analysis because, as is symptomatic of how power and privilege work, they are often indiscernible and thereby unconscious to the people who have them, including white teachers.

Thus, rather than accentuating the enduring presence and tragic complexities of oppression, those of us committed to a pedagogical parrhesia that is grounded in and built on the idea of guiding our students to "speak truth to power" must start speaking *about* power. Pedagogically parrhesiastic educators must pointedly situate the ways in which we are powered-over [dominated by systems and individuals], powered-to [connected to forms of power that, in turn, dominate others], and powered-from [the capacity to resist domination].[6] As Stokely challenged his audience to disrupt their reliance on freedom as an implicit and isolated discourse for race, racialization, and racial justice, we, as educators must disrupt our reliance on talking about oppression in implicit and isolated ways in pursuit of emancipation. In effect, our ability to refuse isolated pedagogies of oppression by engaging pedagogies of power will invite students of all privileges to partake in the pursuit and creation of an emancipated democracy that forewarns all forms of power, "move over, or we're gonna' move on over you."[7]

Protest-In-Practice

The ways in which we pragmatically engage power in our teaching and learning will require us to employ reflexive, deconstructive, and reconstructive techniques in our planning, preparation, instruction, and questioning. In their lesson-planning or assessment-planning processes, teachers who want to restructure power dynamics must feel comfortable openly discussing the role and dynamic of power in the classroom with grade team leaders, mentoring teachers, co-teachers, assistant teachers, teaching residents, or grade team partners. Several steps you can take to do this work are as follows:

1. Be bold, *frank and dangerous*—parrhesiastic values, and ask the question, what would be the benefits to our group if we shared or deconstructed power?
2. Remind yourself and remind your colleagues that power is not a finite and fixed paradigm; rather, it can be infinite, expanded, inclusive, and shared amongst many folx within a community.
3. Create your own personal maps of power and privilege by considering how your own visible and invisible identities, community memberships, allegiances, and lived experiences provide or deny you access and power.
4. Compare your personal maps and consider where you overlap and where you may unintentionally exert power over one another.
5. In the instructional planning process, if there are two or more educators within the classroom, ideate and annotate [in writing on lesson plans] the ways you all can share "power with" each other instead of "power over" each other.
6. Make a list of teaching and power agreements—I tend to call these *vows*.
7. Invite each other to monitor the agreements and be courageous enough to intervene, by "calling in"[8] if the other is not practicing them. This "calling in" should not be interruptive, disruptive, or rude. Instead, it should be warm though resolute, through post-it notes, or a whisper, or during an independent student-work moment, or

through any other shared protocol that is invisible to the student eye or clearly contextualized for students.

This work of calling each other to task may be immensely uncomfortable at moments, but it is necessary discomfort for rethinking, restructuring, and rewriting power dynamics within communities, particularly within classrooms. And folx of color, particularly Black and brown educators, should not be the only courageous ones to monitor power agreements. White teachers, in particular, should monitor the agreements. Think of speaking as a pie graph and take a mental note of who is eating most of the pie, and who is not.

A few years ago, Beth, a white mentor teacher with two teaching residents in her classroom, came to me concerned that Leslie, one of her teaching residents, was constantly talking over or rephrasing what Anna, her other teaching resident, had just said to students. "It's like she forgets that she is also learning how to teach and she is so busy making sure the kids hear it the way she wants them to hear it that she doesn't realize that she's bulldozing Anna." I asked her what she had done to address the problem and she told me she had recorded the dynamic and showed it to the two residents. She said they both agreed it was a problem, but that it kept happening. "I think I am just going to separate them so that they can each practice uninhibited on their own," she told me.

I agreed that was an option but asked her to consider the anti-Black message that was being sent to young people. Leslie, an Asian-American woman, was repeatedly talking over and rephrasing Anna, a Black woman. I encouraged Beth to revisit the vows they had each created at the beginning of the year and consider where Leslie was exerting her power over Anna, and most importantly, *why* Leslie might be exerting power over Anna. Together, they re-reviewed the video, this time with their personal power maps and vows in hand. Leslie came to the conclusion that her "desire to do it her way" was sending a really harmful message to the young people and undermining the vows the team had created. Together, they came up with a new way for Anna and Beth to call Leslie in, in real time, when she was exerting power over Anna. It is critical in these moments to pause and consider how historical racial dynamics and tensions between groups of folx—consciously and unconsciously, often seeded from conversations in the home—might be influencing the power dynamics of classrooms.

As teachers committed to being and doing community, we must be proactive about the ways in which we amplify the power of people who are habitually at the margins of conversations in our classrooms, as in the world. Centering folx who are traditionally at the margin is not only about inviting voices when the conversation, activity, or theme pertains to an area that impacts those at the margin. This is a gross misuse of identity and lived knowledge as a fetishized learning tool for the sake of whiteness, and is not the role of Black and brown colleagues or students. Instead, centering folx who are traditionally at the margin is about inviting voices, meaningfully and impactfully, in all conversations, all themes, and all areas as a mechanism to deconstruct and *abolish* the power-hoarding of whiteness in pedagogical spaces.

For Teachers of Color

Here are a handful of sentence starters for teachers of color, who recognize when you [or your students] have been and/or are being marginalized by a white colleague or co-teacher within the classroom community:

1. "When you all heard Ms./Mr./Mx.[9]_____ say that, did anyone have a reaction? Because what came up for me was _____."
2. "Can you say that differently? I'm wondering if there is an alternative way to word it."
3. "I just heard _____. I am going to push you, and the rest of the class to consider _____."
4. "In my experience, as a person of color, _____."

For White Teachers

On the other hand, here are a handful of sentence starters for white teachers to intentionally yield space for the leadership of historically marginalized teachers and students. When it is a collegial invitation of a co-teacher, assistant teacher, or resident, it would be wise to plan the invitation, so you are not intentionally or unintentionally utilizing your positional power as a "cold call" invitation. The public invitation is intended to establish in the minds of students, namely white students, that there is shared and distributed power in leadership within the classroom.

1. "Ms./Mr./Mx. _____, how about you lead this next portion, and I'm going to circulate the room."
2. "There are so many different ways you can understand _____. Ms./Mr./Mx._____, would you like to introduce us to alternative/additional/varying ways of understanding _____."
3. "I just heard you say _____. I am going to yield to Ms./Mr./Mx. _____, to lead/facilitate us make meaning of that."
4. "In my experience, _____. Ms./Mr./Mx. _____, would you be willing to share your experience?"
5. "I noticed a few reactions when I said _____. I'm going to ask if anyone would like to share what their reaction was in response to."

Power Between Teachers and Students

The relationships between co-teachers are complicated, but sometimes we are so worried about "losing power" that we miss chances to help students see hidden power systems. Make sure your discussions of power go further than yourselves as colleagues to the students. When developmentally appropriate, consider: how are your students "at the table"? How are their priorities, assets, and skills driving the discussion? How are you sharing power with students? One way to engage students directly is to reframe questions about oppression and identity through a power-framework. For example:

1. What identities and groups of people have had access to power within our society?
2. How did those identities and groups secure their power?
3. What, then, does that mean about identities and groups of power who were powered-over, or had access to *less* power?
4. What systems in our society have allowed for this power imbalance to occur today?
5. How do you experience those systems of power in your lives outside of school?
6. How are those systems of power playing out in our classroom?
7. When do you feel like you can call out systems of power in your lives?
8. *For younger students:* do you feel like you can speak up and be honest when you feel like people—adults and sometimes, even other kids—are using power against you?
9. How might we interrupt and demolish those systems of power in our lives?
10. How might we interrupt and demolish those systems of power in our classroom?

Power-sharing starts from the very first day of the school year. Traditionally, before the school year starts, teachers often imagine their ideal learning environment and then begin the school year by working with students to establish classroom "contracts" that will support the students to fit into that ideal environment. In our attempt to interrupt power dynamics, contractual language between teachers and students is inherently problematic, particularly when white teachers are creating contracts with Black and brown students. Cultivating a classroom for pedagogical protest is not about creating terms and conditions for compliance imposed on the minds and bodies of students. Classrooms committed to pedagogical protest are guided by communal agreements and community vows that hold teachers as accountable for their uses and misuses of power as they hold students accountable. For students who struggle to meet the agreed upon expectations and pledges, teachers will frequently take corrective actions to redirect those students. For example, when John fails to remain seated to complete his worksheet, John's teacher will set a small goal with John. If John can complete one problem today and two tomorrow, they have made progress toward the ideal classroom environment. In this example, John's energy level is seen as a deficit to be overcome. In a power-sharing classroom guided by agreements and vows, not terms and conditions, the teacher, instead of imagining the ideal learning environment, considers the assets of the young people in the space and codesigns the environment around those. So, if John was going to be in the class and is a young person who engages best when on the move, the teacher would see John's energy as an asset and create learning sprints, thinking walks, or other physical ways for John to engage in the content. One way a teacher can begin to design a classroom with power-sharing is to know the following about students before co-creating classroom expectations, co-designing classroom structures, and co-developing classroom language:

1. Who are the students in my classroom?
2. When have they felt most proud of themselves?
3. What have they felt most at ease?
4. When have they felt the least successful?
5. What was an emotionally uncomfortable moment in their lives?

Beyond these general pedagogical strategies, teachers who wish to engage in a culture of power-sharing must design lessons, teaching moves, informal and formal assessments, checks for understanding, and in-class activities to include multiple voices and perspectives at the core, not at the periphery. As you plan, ensure that you begin with the voices and lived knowledge of your students, and that you have marked moments throughout the lesson when you intentionally invite students, namely of historically marginalized and oppressed identities, to step forward to lead conversations. This is not only about students, let us be *very clear*. If you are a white teacher, and your co-teacher, resident, or assistant teacher has less power in the school community because of role, positional status, or less sociopolitical and sociocultural power based on the social identities of race, gender, sexuality, physical ability status, or other embodied and lived identities, then invite that person to lead. By recognizing that power dynamics are always present, even when you are well-meaning and have well-meaning intentions, you will be more cognizant of deconstructing your own use of power by doing more listening than speaking. One powerful way to do this is to redefine expertise.

1. What would it look like for young people to grade one another's work?
2. What would it look like for young people to design assessment?
3. What would it look like for young people to facilitate discussion?
4. What would it look like for young people to provide me feedback regularly?

All of these things are possible if we recognize that knowledge and expertise come in many forms and that a young person, for example, might be better suited to give feedback on the relatability of their peers writing than a teacher.

Feedback and assessment are areas in particular where power dynamics are grossly imbalanced. Even though we know that instruction and learning are hyper local, personal, and applicable, too often we purchase or design assessment that is generic, impersonal, and inaccessible. In assessment design, we tend to focus on what we are assessing rather than why we are assessing. Teachers committed to a pedagogy of protest and power-sharing engage their young people in assessment analysis and design.

Once, when I was interviewing an aspiring teacher, I asked her what a successful classroom looked and sounded like. She responded, in part:

> When I was interning at a charter school last summer, I heard the word "urgency" all the time. Teachers were always being told to show urgency. I remember hearing about how the work was too important to approach with anything but urgency. We were always pushing through lessons, trying new things, and asking kids to get to the end faster. I've been thinking about that a lot. I think maybe the work is too important for "urgency". I think a good classroom moves slowly and intentionally and makes sure that all students are a part of the learning.

A teacher who loves students holds space for struggle and authentic learning. A teacher who loves students slows down long enough to share power with them. When I was a fifth-grade teacher and leading a drill-and-kill test preparation after school class for the third year in a row, I looked out at a sea of bored Black and Brown faces endlessly bubbling in a spreadsheet. I stopped the class and said, "Well, after weeks of doing this exercise, you have seen the same types of questions over and over again. What do these questions tell you about the people who make these tests? What do they think is important?" This was the first day of my reimagined test preparation; if we were required to spend hours on top of hours practicing for a disempowering test, then we were also going to analyze rubrics, analyze question types, and figure out what these State tests told us about the people in power. I could not free my students from taking the tests, but I could help make their own systems of power and oppression more transparent. Pedagogically parrhesiastic educators know that intentionally antiracist, anti-oppressive, power-deconstructing, and radically human(e) assessment design, implementation, and evaluation can help to empower children. For assessment to be a tool of protest and liberation, teachers must ask themselves:

1. Does this assessment allow for more than one way of knowing, and give young people a chance to demonstrate broad accessible knowledge, content specific knowledge, and skills?
2. Does this assessment allow students to showcase their learning, progress, and genius in multiple ways?
3. Does this assessment provide clear data that showcases the individuality, lived-experiences, expertise, and intellect of each student in a way that supports teachers to tailor instruction to specific learners?

We cannot disrupt what we are unwilling to name. But, if we can name power dynamics, create tools to redistribute power, and interrupt ourselves when we fall into dangerous patterns, we can begin to disrupt oppression at its macro and micro levels. Our disruption is the seed for deconstruction, and our deconstruction offers us hope for reimagination.

Notes

1. Stokely Carmichael and Charles V. Hamilton. (1967). *Black Power: The Politics of Liberation in America.* New York: Vintage, 50.
2. Victoria J. Gallagher. (2001). "Black Power in Berkeley: Postmodern Constructions in the Rhetoric of Stokely Carmichael." *Quarterly Journal of Speech*, vol. 87, no. 2: 145.

3. Stokely Carmichael (Kwame Ture). (2007). *Stokely Speaks: From Black Power to Pan-Africanism*. Chicago, IL: Lawrence Hill Books, 51.
4. Gallagher, 152.
5. Gallagher, 153.
6. Bret Kloos, Jean Hill, Elizabeth Thomas, Abraham Wandersman, Maurice Elias, and James Dalton. (2012). *Community Psychology: Linking Individuals and Communities*. Boston, MA: Wadsworth Cengage.
7. Ture, 60.
8. "Calling in" is essentially a mechanism to invite a moment/person of oppression to cease by acknowledging the expansiveness of conscious and unconscious/intentional and unintentional oppressive tendencies and guiding that moment/person to see why the thoughts/words/actions are harmful to marginalized folx and how to address them. While the public act of "calling out" has its place, "calling in" as an individual, non-embarrassing act can often yield more sustainable transformed thoughts/words/actions.
9. Mx., pronounced as "mix," is a respectability title as more folx openly identify as transgender, gender-nonconforming, agender, and nonbinary—and therefore the use of miss, missus, and mister.

6

Just Another Day: Talk About the Everydayness of Race

Protest-in-Context

the sun awakens and the moon sleeps
their name unknown to the reel
their story untold by the witnesses
they are called by their names before they were they
   before the passage
   before the soul found rest
   before the brain and body agreed
they belong to Black
ours, but we do not accept them
bruised skin, discolored lips
embodied terror
   male
   female
   they
   them

both
neither
we look right through them
we disrobe them of the right to be human
 unclothed from the rite to be a soul
we mask them to not see them
but they belongs to Black
ours, but we do not want them
just another day
 being Black
the sun sleeps and the moon awakens
silence on the streets
kids in beds
noise abounds, all around
beyond, within, above, beneath, alongside
deafening terror
 she screams
 cries for defense
 screams for salvation
silent to us
 we are tough until its them
they belong to Black
ours, but we do not accept them
unseen, unheard, unvalued
we talk over them
 our sainted ones
we use them to not see them
 our sainted ones
but she belongs to Black
ours, but we do not want her
just another day
 being Black
the sun stalls and the moon delays
 no darkness
 no light

just another day
being Black
no names, no stories, no noises
silence
shadows
stillness
stupor
just another day
being Black
we do not know the future
but, in spirit, we do
persecution
poverty
pain
just another day
being Black
we are but a replica of the past
and, inseparable from it
suffering
surviving
stretching
just another day
being Black
today undefined
what relief
but, not undefiled
what sorrow
just another day
them
her
him
us
just another day
being Black

—Robert S. Harvey

Incidents such as Amy Cooper's false accusations against a Black man in New York City's Central Park, and the racial-capitalist paternalism of Tom Austin in a Minneapolis gym, both captured by citizen journalism, tend to shade racist acts with an undeniable exceptionalism that overshadows the everydayness of racism in this country. With social media stories and policy body camera footage of bloodied and murdered Black bodies holding the brevity of our attention through headlines of news reels for a few weeks at a time, exceptionalizing the predictability and triteness of what it means to be a Black or brown, queer or economically vulnerable person in this nation, white folx are allowed to experience reprieves from their quotidian racism. While the refrain "Say Their Names" has become an echoing soundtrack on the streets, in protests, in memorials, and in classrooms, there are so many other names we have not said. From the markedly genius performativity of Beyoncé Knowles-Carter and Serena Williams to the respectability allure of President Barack Obama and Oprah Winfrey, the white gaze under which Black and brown folx live imposes a type of pressure on *all* Black and brown folx to realize that which is reserved for the one-percent.

It's not that the gaze of whiteness only wants to limit the expansiveness of the Black and brown experience, it's that it wants to limit the expansiveness of success through a white-centric, capitalist, competitive framework where the markers of that success are money, properties, and power. It is why we subconsciously hyper-hail the futuristic aspirations of young people as they assert, "I want to be a basketball player," and "I want to be the president," or "I want to be an astronaut." In the shadowiness of our deaths in the streets and in the opulence of our attainments on artistic, athletic, financial, and political stages, exceptionalism limits our access to freedom, and thus limits the names our students know, say, and esteem. So many names unknown, yet names that matter. So many stories untold, yet stories that matter. And, in teaching and learning communities across this nation, we often fail to talk about the everydayness of race and racism—an *everydayness* that is not boisterous, noisy, or sensational, but discreet, normalized, insidious, and easy.

To begin with everydayness as entrée, as concept, as framing is to presume that we are all conscious of the everyday—that is, sentient of what it means to do life with cognizance of one's humanity, one's movement in the world, and one's sense of being unlike those with access to power. *Everydayness.* It is a concept describing the day-to-day "approach to the concept of freedom as long as we realize that conduct it not [ours] alone, but [ours] in response to, and drawing responses from, others."[1] For Black and brown folx, queer and economically vulnerable folx, our everyday interactions with ourselves and others, namely white others, is a commonplace practice of pursuing freedom that we have yet to attain beyond our imaginings. Everydayness is as much a practice of hopeful possibilities as it is a practice of dangerous criticality—critical of ourselves for not being the exceptional, and critical of our white others for creating the conditions to presume that freedom is only earmarked for the exceptional. Everydayness is the enunciation of being fully human without our names being known, without our stories being told, without our dreams being manifested, and without our emancipation being taken seriously. It is a complicated easiness and an embodied discontent in relationship and in tension with each other, both seeking to consume the reserve of our consciousness. This tension, then, for educators driven by the notion of pedagogical protest is that, when we are conscious of race and *everydayness*, we deliberately utilize our classrooms to complicate the politics of who matters and what stories are told. In classrooms led and facilitated by Black and brown educators, this is particularly our responsibility in that "we who are dark can see America in a way that white Americans cannot."[2] We see America in its everydayness.

If we candidly grappled with why race and racism is so complicated to address, resist, and deconstruct, we would have to concede that, in part, it is from a lack of framing: that race is an everyday construct that is as much individual as it is communal; that race—as experienced in our individual daily lives—is the aggregate of our myriad mundane thoughts, words, and actions; and that the everydayness of race is often underacknowledged and, therefore, conceals the problematic comings and goings of white folx. At the end of the chapter, "Of the Sons of Master and Man," W.E.B. du Bois elucidates the aforementioned when he writes:

> But after all that has been said on these more tangible matters of human contact, there still remains a part essential to a proper description of the South which it is difficult to describe or fix in terms easily understood by strangers. It is, in fine, the thousand and one little actions which go to make up life. In any community or nation it is these little things which are most elusive to grasp and yet most essential to any clear conception of the group life taken as a whole.[3]

This is a piercing clarion call for educators to create the classroom conditions necessary for naming and unpacking the everydayness of race and racism with students. Du Bois, after all, offers us the sense "that one could not adequately understand racism in America unless one understood how racist practices were threaded through mundane, daily existence."[4] White educators' avoidance to create these conditions might be related to a perceived fear of vulnerability, a fear of saying the wrong things, a fear of being seen as racist, a fear of exposing young people to *triggering and traumatizing* realities, or a fear of the unknown borne of what it means to engage young people about complicated topics. However, when educators circumvent the everydayness of race and racism in the classroom, they are actually embodying what Black and brown folx know about America already—it is a nation, in so many ways, built on avoiding its own truths and its complicity in oppression. In effect, avoidance of everydayness is engagement with everydayness.

In order to understand the hypervigilant surveillance of Black and brown bodies in disinvested and under-resourced communities, we must analyze the daily surveillance of bodies in hallways and classrooms, in dress codes and hairstyles. To make meaning of "hands up, don't move" policing in the streets, we must scrutinize the "be still, stop talking" classroom culture perpetuated in the name of "maintaining order so things don't get out of hand." We must dissect the ways in which we acclaim the dreams of young people that subscribe to conventionally linear pathways, and the skepticism we preserve when those dreams transcend linearity. We must consider the frameworks we employ as criteria for success—in our classrooms, in community, and beyond—and the rubrics we utilize to measure achievement.

As we pause and become conscious of the everyday racism that goes unaddressed and unacknowledged in lieu of our hyper-attentiveness to the exceptional, we might find ourselves suffocating on the smog of that we have been socialized to disregard—or, even more problematically, socialized to accept as inbuilt to the ways our world should operate. That smog of everyday racism, everyday inequity, and everyday oppression, Beverly Daniel Tatum writes, "is so thick it is visible, other times it is less apparent, but always, day in and day out, we are breathing it in."[5] Per Tatum's analysis, then, it befits us—as pedagogical parrhesiastics—to lessen our focus on racial exceptionalism and sensational racism, and to increase our emphasis on the everyday smog that unreflexively forms and informs the meaning-making of our students. That is, we are compelled to the analytical everydayness work of shepherding our students to consciously make sense of their critical consumption of words, images, definitions, symbols, structures, systems, rules, and policies that permeate the ways they think about and do their humanity. In a national climate with a clear insatiability for the racial macro, how do we cultivate a classroom for young people who take seriously the racial micro? Doing so begins the pedagogical process of closing the individual and communal floodgate that privileges the "exceptional Negro" complex which presumes that Blackness must exceptional—in a divergent, unprecedented, and peculiar sense—in order to be esteemed.

By taking seriously the racial-micro, the everydayness of race and racism, it begins the healing process of centuries of whiteness pitting Black folx against Black folx, brown folx against brown folx, and other marginalized folx against each other by suggesting that one type of lived experience—the type that meets the public criteria for sensational—is somehow exempt from everyday subjugation, and therefore, transcends systemic oppression. In pitting oppressed people against each other, on the basis of exceptionalism versus everydayness, racist white folx and the structures they manage can hold concurrently, a spoken and unspoken, named and unnamed disdain for daily, commonplace Blackness and Black folx alongside an approbation of Black one percenters and Blackness in its elite, capitalist forms. It is this unconsciousness duality, which is often the culprit behind white folx who say: "You're nothing like other Black people that I've encountered" as if their experience of the *other Black people* was episodic of a brand of Blackness that should cease to exist. When educators, namely white ones, make seemingly inconsequential comments akin to, "You are so articulate," "I love the way you tuck your shirt in," "I appreciate that you know how to zip your lips when we are working independently," they perpetuate racial inequalities at a systemic level.

However, when we take seriously the racial micro, the everydayness of race and racism, we may begin a healing process. For our young people in America—Black, brown, queer, and economically vulnerable—the lived experiences, oppressions, and stories of everydayness are as problematic as the exceptional. Therefore, we—pedagogical parrhesiastic educators—must analyze everydayness as not only a space in which race and racism happens, but also as a point of praxis for how race and racism happens. The everyday, in this sense, is not merely a site for pedagogical parrhesia, because everydayness itself plays an overriding role in creating, sustaining, and/or deconstructing boundaries of race and racism. Of course, we must not diminish the weight or lose sight of the ways in which the sensational nature of race and racism impacts the lived experiences of Black and brown young people, particularly in the hyperviolent and bloodied streets from the frequency of police murders. Much the same, we must not overlook, underprivilege, or deny the psychological and emotional impact of our students' ordinary encounters with racism as they navigate their identities and personhood in our classrooms. The questions, then, for us as educators are: how do we talk and teach about the daily, unromantic, everydayness of race and racism with young people in our classrooms? How do we, as teachers, create and hold space to learn from the everyday expertise of our young people's families, lived experiences, and social-cultural knowledge? How do we harness the everyday, inherent human exceptionalism of those nearest to us—not capitalist success stories but parents and grandparents, caregivers and clergy, teachers and coaches, mentors and friends—in our pedagogy?

Protest-in-Practice

Several years ago, while taking prospective teachers on school tours, I began noticing how many classrooms were named after colleges; not just any colleges, but the most exclusive, restrictive, historically white colleges in the nation. I lost count of how many classrooms were named after the Ivy Leagues and the Seven Sisters—historically white, all women's colleges in the Northeastern United States—and I could tally on one hand the number of classrooms named after local city colleges, public universities, historically Black colleges and universities (HBCUs), and Hispanic-serving institutions (HSIs).[6] One school we visited, however, deviated from this trend by naming its classrooms after "local heroes." Despite the famous musical, activist, and culinary history of the local community, I did not recognize the names of any of these heroes. When I asked our tour guide to tell us more about them, she told me that the heroes were all graduates of the network who had gone on to prestigious colleges. Both of these examples left me wondering how we define success for our young people. How do we encourage Black and brown students to recognize the very real, everyday accomplishments of, say, a neighbor who is working while attending community college full time, without inadvertently telling them that more traditionally prestigious goals are out of reach?

Defining "Success"

One strategy is to work with students to set clear definitions of words like "hero" and "success," definitions that invite everydayness, accessibility, and proximity. You can do this by asking students:

1. Who do you consider successful? On the other hand, what do you consider unsuccessful?
2. Why do you believe those are the indicators of success?
3. Who is the most successful person you know personally?
4. Who is someone who has made *your life* a better life?
5. Who is someone who has made the world a better place?
6. Who is a person in the community who has made something change for the better?
7. Who is a person who has accomplished something great?
8. Who is someone you know who has accomplished something great?

Once students have named their people (emphasis on *their*), and explained why they selected each of their people, follow up by asking them:

1. How would you describe this person?
2. What do they do and say that makes you know they are successful?

3. What character traits do they have?
4. What work and or learning have they done to get them where they are today?

As a class, you can then find common patterns in the responses and generate a list of what makes success or what makes a hero. For the rest of the school year, students can use the created criteria to identify everyday heroes and proximate successes, along with celebrity heroes. They can also adapt and change the criteria as they learn about family, historical figures, community members, and celebrities who might change their thinking. Even as we support young people to find heroes and set goals, we must give them tools to make the everydayness of racism transparent. If they can clearly identify, articulate, and challenge the bigotry they are facing, students will be more equipped to live according to qualities they find heroic and meet their goals (emphasis, again, on *they* and *their*).

When training aspiring teachers, I spend the first four weeks working with the candidates to create a framework to talk about race and racism. We watch clips from school board meetings, read legislation, and watch videos of instruction and ask ourselves, "Where do we see racism here?" For each primary source we analyze, we identify evidence of internal, social, and systemic racism. In one video we watched recently, a white mother in Carmel, New York,[7] is expressing anger with the School Board's decision to adopt a curriculum grounded in Critical Race Theory. In her impassioned speech, she shows evidence of multiple layers of racism. For example, one teaching candidate pointed out the woman's claim that she has a right to weigh in on curricular decisions because, among other things, she pays for the chairs the Board members sit on. In that example, we discussed the systemic racism that comes from property taxes funding schools; we talked about the internalized superiority she showed when she suggested her money bought her access; and we considered the social racism on display when she reduced the Latina deputy superintendent's worth to her salary.

Through daily practice with examples like this, teaching candidates grow accustomed to analyzing the world through this lens. At first, they are often able to point out exaggerated and subtle shows of racism but lack the language or historical context to explain what makes the example racist. Even when they can tell me why they think examples are racist, they tend to notice the social or interpersonal aspects of racism much more easily than the internal and systemic. But through practice, it becomes a part of their everyday language to point out all of the layers of racism in their daily encounters. This is an important exercise for aspiring teachers because it gives them a starting point for questioning and challenging everyday racism.

Imagine if these teachers could bring this practice into their classrooms. If they could teach students about the internal, social, and systemic layers of racism and then ask young people to consider how they see those pieces at play in their daily lives and learnings, teachers would be laying the groundwork for future activists. To do this, teachers should:

1. **Define the layers of racism**

    It is important to start with common language. There are many articles and resources to help you define these layers of racism. Whichever tool you choose, in the end, young people should be able to define systemic racism as having to do with official laws and policies that grant or deny access based on race, social racism as the ways in which individuals who are granted systemic power exert their authority over others, and internalized racism as ways that those with systemic power pass judgement or make assumption about those without systemic power.

2. **Look at clear examples from national events**

    While we do not want to limit the conversation about racism to only the events that make national headlines, those are often the most obvious to examine when using this framework for the first time. Whether dissecting the layers of racism in a police brutality case or a school segregation debate, make sure students are looking for evidence for each layer of racism. They can dissect quotes from people involved, read the language used in news stories, and read laws or claims of legal precedent. As they do this, they should be asking:

    a. What systems were in place that allowed this outcome?
    b. What human interactions allowed this to happen?
    c. What assumptions were/are people involved making and how do I know?

3. **Analyze more subtle historical or local examples**

    Once students can dissect overtly racist examples, it will be much easier for them to apply this process to less obvious examples like school policies, conversations overheard on their way to school, articles about local community efforts, historical events, college acceptance rates, and so on.

4. **Pull examples from personal context**.

    The most difficult step is the one in which students now apply this framework to their everyday lives, asking themselves:

    a. How does my racial identity factor into what just happened to me?
    b. What do statistics disaggregated along racial lines suggest the outcomes will be?
    c. How can I counter the social and systemic racism that the data tells me I will or did experience in this moment?

Once we are able call out the racist ways we are provided or denied access in any given moment, it will be much easier to consider new ways of doing and being.

Notes

1. Webb Keane. (2014). "Freedom, Reflexivity, and the Sheer Everydayness of Ethics." *HAU: Journal of Ethnographic Theory*, vol. 4, no. 1: 453.
2. W.E.B. du Bois. ([1926]1986). "Criteria of Negro Art." *Writings*, edited by W.E.B. du Bois. New York: Literary Classics of the United States, 993.
3. W.E.B. du Bois. ([1903]1995). *The Souls of Black Folk*. New York: Signet Classic, 203.
4. Andrew Smith. (2015). "Rethinking the 'Everyday' in 'Ethnicity and Everyday Life.'" *Ethnic and Racial Studies*, vol. 38, no. 7: 1147.
5. Beverly Daniels Tatum. (2004). "Defining Racism: Can We Talk?" *Race, Class, and Gender in the United States, Sixth Edition*, edited by Paula S. Rothenberg. New York: Worth Publishers, 126.
6. Hispanic-serving Institutions (HSIs) is a federal designation of the United States government conceived in the early 1990s to recognize the growing number of Latinx students in higher education. Unlike historically Black colleges and universities (HBCUs) and tribal colleges, HSIs were not founded on the basis of serving Latinx students; the designation is fundamentally an indicator of Latinx enrollment. This designation can pose significant pedagogical challenges, in large part, because any higher education institution can designate itself as an HIS once Latinx enrollment meets or surpasses a 25 percent threshold, *regardless* of whether the institution intentionally designs for, programs toward, or strategically engages the distinct realities of Latinx students.
7. The Indicrat. (2021). *Angry Mom Blasts Critical Race Theory at School Board Meeting - New York*. YouTube. Retrieved from: https://www.youtube.com/watch?v=py5MsL_i2cl.

7

How Does It Feel to *Not* Be a Problem? Talk About Whiteness

Protest-in-Context

> *Whiteness, the unremarked abyss shadowing the American soul.*
> *Whiteness, the unquestioned note defining what it means to sing America.*
> *Whiteness, the uninterrogated witness privy to America's guilt.*

And yet, Blackness—the sun-bronzed and fire-blazoned politic of enduring and blooming, working and singing, escaping and building, creating and writing, crying and hoping—is narrativized through a lens of unremarked, unquestioned, and uninterrogated whiteness as America's problem. Think of the myriad ways we offhandedly color blackness as the problematic underside of a binary when we invoke the imagery of black/white, darkness/light, evil/good, filthy/clean, sadness/joy, and damnable/redemptive. In effect, this coloring of blackness radically forms and informs why Black folx are seen, heard, and experienced as a problem in this nation. In the opening of "Of

DOI: 10.4324/9781003183365-7

Our Spiritual Strivings," W.E.B. du Bois illumes what it means for Blackness to be experienced as a problem by the white gaze:

> Between me and the other world there is an unasked question: unasked by some through feelings of delicacy; by others through the difficult of rightly framing it. All, nevertheless, flutter round it. They approach me in a half-hesitant sort of way, eye me curiously or compassionately, and then, instead of saying directly, How does it feel to be a problem? they say, I know an excellent colored man in my town; or, I fought at Mechanicsville; or, Do not these Southern outrages make your blood boil? At these I smile, or am interest, or reduce the boiling to a simmer, as the occasion may require. To the real question, How does it feel to be a problem? I answer seldom a word.[1]

Inherent, though unwritten, in du Bois' analysis of what it means to be perceived as a problem is that "the other world," the world of whiteness—through its gaze toward Blackness and Black bodies—has never had to experience what it means to be perceived as a problem. Why, you ask? Because the normalization of whiteness and the impenetrable methods of protecting itself—legally, judicially, economically, politically, socially, and pedagogically—are cornerstones of the ways in which institutions are systematically designed to function in the United States. "We live in a society where default whiteness goes unremarked—no one ever asks it for its passport."[2] Thus, by "othering" whiteness in his use of "other world," du Bois invites a frank, critical, and dangerous dissonance, which compels us to finally (yes, finally, after hundreds and hundreds of years!) become visibly and audibly conscious of the invisibility and silence of whiteness. This consciousness presumes that "the problem is not *of blacks*, but one *of whites*, for it is they who reproduce and maintain the normalizing structures of whiteness that make such a question possible."[3] That would mean, as a practice of pedagogical parrhesia, that unmasking the unremarked, unquestioned, uninterrogated whiteness is the beginning of the implosion of its gaze, hubris, and presumed dominance.

For two days, August 11–12, 2017, white supremacists and neo-Nazis organized and held a rally, "Unite the Right," in Charlottesville, Virginia. It had one primary goal, according to the organizers, which was to unify the American white national movement. In effect, it was a rally that centered whiteness. Beyond the pageantry of white nationalism and the national grief of witnessing a scene cropped out of the 1960s, Charlottesville offered us an opportunity to pull back the curtain on the insidious culture, economic incentive, political utility, and historical continuity of racism still alive in America. It is a type of racism that can only be explained by understanding whiteness as a structural system at the foundation of this nation. Abandoning their white hoods as seeming relics of a former species of white hate, white folx carried torches and paraded toward a monument of Robert E. Lee, the embodiment of the Confederate Army during the Civil War. While the Alt Right, Klu Klux Klan, and neo-Nazis are the most lethal extension of racism embodied, whiteness and white supremacy are diffusive, pervasive, and everywhere. Yes, everywhere. How? Because white supremacy is America's birth defect, coded in the very structural foundation of our republic, and it has made one of its homes in schools and classrooms all across the nation.

What is whiteness, you ask? Whiteness refers to the structural logic and systemic culture of white folx [and those who align and ascribe to whiteness as the standard for all racial and cultural identities], not simply skin color or ancestry. Before we can go any further, it is critical to pause and internalize that distinction between people *being white*—a socially constructed racial category with no biological/scientific foundation, like every other socially constructed racial category—and *whiteness*, the devouring social-political-ethical construct with real, experienced, embodied, violent effects on Black, brown, and non-white folx. Whereas *being white* is a socially constructed labeling, *whiteness* is social-political-ethical embodiment grounded in historical oppression and colonialization, ideological and political supremacy, systemic economic inequity, and the literal subjugation of non-white bodies and communities. Moreover, it endures as a social-political-ethical privilege and dominance that is lived out in ways that diminish the inherent humanity and personhood of Black, brown, and non-white folx. It is a gaze, a hue, a coloring, a social mechanism whereby all folx, involuntarily, are compared to whiteness as the standard for being. Whiteness is a logic that governs our lives, forges ways of thinking, and produces frameworks of meaning. White supremacist logic silences and works against the legitimacy of non-white equality and belonging, namely Black being, Black equality, and Black belonging. That is to say, notions like "Black Lives Matter" are only requisite when situated against the pervasive logic that whiteness inherently matters in the fabric of our nation. Not only matters, but also has never been question as mattering. Not only has never been question as mattering, but also has never been a problem.

As an indictment of whiteness, particularly wedded to patriarchy, the tasks of confronting, defining, and deconstructing whiteness are, within the context of pedagogical parrhesia, vital to the struggles of frankness, criticism, and, in particular, danger. If danger is, in fact, our willingness to risk likeability and diminish one's own power, privilege, or popularity in order to address any thought, word, or deed that intentionally or unintentionally underprivileges or subjugates folx, particularly Black folx (as addressed in Chapter 1), then confronting whiteness in our pedagogy is the utmost struggle. In other words, it could be argued that an educator cannot do pedagogical parrhesia, in any form, without a frank and critical confrontation of whiteness, a confrontation borne of [moral] duty and hope rather than guilt-laden coercion. This is particularly the case for white educators in classrooms full of Black and brown young folx, white educators who claim to be committed to pedagogical protest, emancipating learning, and antiracist pursuits. bell hooks notes:

> …whether they are able to enact it as a lived practice or not, many white folks active in anti-racist struggle today are able to acknowledge that all whites (as well as everyone else within white supremacist culture) have learned to overvalue "whiteness" even as they simultaneously learn to devalue blackness. They understand the need, at least intellectually, to alter their thinking. Central to this process of unlearning white supremacist attitudes and values is the deconstruction of the category of "whiteness."[4]

At the core of hooks' argument is the learned overvaluing of whiteness, which has mutated into a passive belief in, tolerance of, and complicity with whiteness as a mainstream American construct that eludes interrogation, particularly in classrooms. Therein lies the paradox of undertaking antiracist, anti-oppressive pedagogical work—the unstated but inferred presumption that one can do antiracist work without attending to the notion of whiteness, the ways it asserts control, and its function as the systematic nemesis of Blackness, brownness, and non-whiteness. Without attending to whiteness in our classrooms, particularly when students are in the more malleable stages of cognitive development, we negligently engender spaces that shape teenagers and young adults who are appalled, outraged, and traumatized—in a passive sense—when they are forced to confront their whiteness and/or their complicit in whiteness.

> Usually, white students respond with naïve amazement that black people critically assess white people from a standpoint where "whiteness" is the privileged signifier. Their amazement that black watch white people with a critical "ethnographic" gaze, is itself an expression of

racism ... They have a deep emotional investment in the myth of "sameness" even as their actions reflect the primacy of whiteness as a sign informing who they are and how they think.⁵

We can still hear this "sameness" address passively in the form of "colorblind"-evocative statements such as "we all bleed the same blood" or "we are all part of the human race." Yet white educators and students rarely espouse this "sameness" when they perceive threats to the stability whiteness, an institution which they have worked so industriously, even unconsciously, to sustain. As offending as it may be, it is rarely surprising to witness the irate, white-supremacist everydayness of white folx who threaten to destabilize Black, brown, and non-white lives over less-than-significant issues. When uninterrogated, unexplored, and unaddressed in classrooms, whiteness is going to white, because "the power they have historically asserted, and even now collectively assert over black people accorded them the right to control the black gaze."⁶ For the sake of a radically equitable and racially inclusive democracy, failing to address whiteness in our classrooms is failing to stop the continued birth of "Miss Ann's," "Karen's," and "Becky's" in the world.⁷

The universal othering of Black, brown, and non-white lives is wholly dehumanizing, particularly in light of the explicit and implicit protection that whiteness is afforded in schools and classrooms when pedagogical saviors take up the space that pedagogical parrhesiastics for emancipatory work. This protection, especially in teaching and learning communities, imperils everyone—Black folx and brown folx, non-white folx and migrant folx, even other white folx who are imperiled by a fraudulent illusion of supremacy and miscomprehension of power over the minds and bodies of folx of color. Educators must come to grips with how the wages of this imperilment, oft experienced in classrooms within communities that suffer profound and politicized disinvestment and underinvestment, is made possible, in part, when *we* disregard the necessary deconstruction of whiteness as we fret and stress over not knowing whether we will "get it right" and so avoid it wholly. (Perfectionism, after all, is a white supremacist value.)

Subsequently, we issue a colonializing license that permits whiteness to function as a subversive influence on how we talk about, think about, and do the work of teaching and learning. In a word, it *enslaves* us. Think about public education, education reform, the opportunity myth, teaching methodologies, and our so-called "best practices." The phantom of whiteness haunts every threaded fabric, from power to policy to praxis to personnel, and, consciously or unconsciously, negates historical truths about the ways in which education, as a politicized institution of the American empire, has chosen to not see and hear Blackness. But, curiously, the insentient pervasiveness of it coerces us as educators to focus so much on "othering" Blackness, brownness, and non-whiteness that we can blind ourselves to the discursive, omnipresent forms of whiteness that inhabit the way we internalize lesson plans and unpack curriculum, the way we think about organizing small groups and differentiating learning access-points, the way we monitor bodies in our classrooms, and the way we assess and grade work.

In order to cultivate the conditions for our classrooms that emancipate our classrooms *from* whiteness, and to deconstruct whiteness as an everyday intentionality that enters into our classrooms with us, we must (yes, must!) deliberately and stridently reject any reduction of whiteness *solely* to confederate flags, racist epithets, cross burnings, bloody lynchings, MAGA hats, congressional insurrections, and/or any other sensational forms of whiteness being white. When we do, we avert the seemingly innocent demonstrations of whiteness in our hallways, classrooms, gymnasiums, playgrounds, and cafeterias, providing a moral cover of the "spirit murdering," in the words of Bettina Love, inflicted on Black, brown, and non-white students every day. Though by no means an exhaustive list, one can perceive the omnipresent, daily forms of whiteness in outdated curricula and intervention methods, zero-tolerance discipline policies, the criminalization of a uniform infractions, white teachers averaging higher salaries as a result of structural access to higher education, white folx occupying instructional leadership roles while Black folx disproportionately occupy "student culture" roles, and legalized voter suppression enabled by racialized and racist politics. But there is hope, because whiteness, as a structural logic and a social-political identity, is a choice that any of us can resist.

It cannot give us hope.
It cannot offer freedom.
It cannot heal our wounds.
It cannot save this democracy.

The question then, is how do we teach about, protest against, and effectively deconstruct whiteness in our classrooms without centering it?

Protest-in-Practice

Before a school community can engage in the work of deconstructing whiteness, they must acknowledge that whiteness as an exclusionary culture is, in fact, a problem. At the start of Peggy McIntosh's article *White Privilege: Unpacking the Invisible Knapsack* she writes, "I was taught to see racism only in individual acts of meanness, not in invisible systems conferring dominance on my group."[8] So, when folx, especially white folx, are asked to see a system of whiteness, this is often new and emotional territory. It is particularly emotional when white folx are asked to see a system of whiteness in a community of Black and brown who are socialized and hegemonized to see whiteness from the youngest ages. White people in this country have been taught to think of ourselves as unique individuals and so struggle to acknowledge that we have a collective culture.

Once while attending a workshop about race and racism, the facilitators asked participants to list the things they loved about their racial cultures. Folx who identified as Black or African American had long lists including music, food, and art. The white people in the room, without being allowed to defer to their ethnic, religious, or regional cultures, struggled to identify shared culture.

The facilitator pushed, "What are some things that all white people have in common that you might not share with people who don't look like you?"

One person said, "We don't have to worry about getting shot when we get pulled over for speeding."

Another added, "We don't usually have to worry about being followed around a store by security."

The facilitator nodded. "I'd call that an aspect of your culture. It's a right to safety."

"I guess," someone said, "But I'm not proud of it. I don't love it."

"You don't?" A Black person asked, incredulous. "You don't love feeling safe? I'd certainly love that."

"I don't love that it's something I have that someone else doesn't," the person responded.

"Well," the facilitator offered, "That was not the question. The question was, 'what do you love about your culture?'"

"I'm not sure I consider that culture," the first speaker responded.

Because society has given white people permission not to see white culture, we do not realize how it shapes our value judgements and our ways of doing and being. In fact, white people are not the only ones subject to not seeing whiteness. Through schooling and other nation-building and democracy-shaping institutions, most (yes, most!) people in this country have been indoctrinated into a white-supremacist system. It can be hard to see through a system that shapes all our lives—hence, whiteness is often reckoned as a smog.

There were several strategies in Chapter 3 that specifically address defining whiteness and testing out other ways of doing and being. Beyond establishing classroom agreements that decenter whiteness and auditing pedagogical materials for whiteness, however, white supremacy must always be called out. It is a tricky balance to talk about and name whiteness without centering it.

In a project I worked on recently with a doctoral cohort, we designed a peer support protocol to address the avoidance of discussing whiteness in schools. One student, a Black member of an equity committee in a predominantly Black and Brown school with a racially diverse staff, was struggling to keep a spotlight on whiteness. After the staff had taken an implicit bias test and engaged in a conversation about white norms, many walked away frustrated, saying things like, "I grew up in the Bronx around all kinds of different people. Race really wasn't an issue," and "I feel a little uncomfortable with all of this. It's almost like reverse racism, making white people feel uncomfortable. I don't like doing that."

A school leader reflected, "It will resonate more for teachers if we give them something concrete to use in their classrooms, if our goal is to be truly responsive." So, we posed the question to the group: *How can school staff continue to be honest about the role of whiteness and its impact on our equity work?*

The simplest answer to this question is to develop a list of white-supremacist values, such as the ones discussed in Chapter 3, and create a set of guiding questions that all community members will use when internalizing curriculum, planning instruction, reviewing student work, creating assessment tools, or designing classroom tasks:

1. What does this task/assignment/work suggest about my values as a teacher?
2. Is my definition of success grounded in the white supremacist values?

3. Do students have choice in how they will demonstrate understanding and growth?
4. Do students have multiple ways to feel successful?
5. Do students have a chance to reflect on their learning?
6. Do students have a chance to reflect on how what they have learned helps them navigate their world?
7. Do students have chance to analyze more than one way of doing or being and consider how those help them interpret content?
8. Do students have a chance to challenge what they are learning?
9. Do students get a chance to analyze which facts they are learning and consider how those facts shape their understanding of truth?

All content areas are subject to whitewashing. Even math, a subject often thought of as objective, neutral, and unprejudiced, is not immune. While it is critical for mathematicians to perform accurate calculations, too many teachers—as a derivative of whiteness—value product over process [which we will talk more about in Chapter 8], teach only one strategy to arrive at a solution, or do not consider how numbers are used to make or alter meaning of the world. What we do with numbers is subject to bias, because all data is subject to stories we choose to tell about the data. Math, science, coding, and STEM teachers should be asking students:

1. What are we solving for and why?
2. How can this math help students navigate their world?
3. How does this formula or process, or the way I'm talking about either, reinforce implicit biases about the world?
4. What data are we collecting and why?
5. What data is missing?
6. What story is this data telling and if we used other data how would the story change?

7. In what ways were our collection methods grounded in how students experience the world? Does that hold true for students from historically marginalized identities?
8. How else might someone quantify this problem?
9. How does this math help us solve a problem?
10. How does this math help us deny a problem?

The work of protesting and deconstructing whiteness should not fall on educators alone. Teachers must lead students through action-oriented learning that allows young people to detect, interrupt, and newly create ways of being and doing that had previously been steeped in whiteness. Once the class has done the work of defining white culture and considering antidotes, in the ways we recommended in Chapter 3, they are ready to consider alternatives:

1. **Work to identify examples of whiteness**

    Whiteness can show up in what we choose to teach, how we choose to teach it, or the systems we create to make our schools and classrooms run. Teachers should work with students to examine school policies, classroom expectations, rubrics, classroom discussion guides, pedagogical materials, and human interactions for evidence of whiteness. They should ask themselves whose culture is valued in each of these areas and why that is the case. They should consider which voices and ways of doing are recognized and celebrated. For example, the students might identify a classroom policy that values the primacy of some individuals over others, like a rewards policy designed by teachers that give privilege to students who complete work early or more efficiently than other students. Students might determine that the policy is grounded in the white supremacist norms of hierarchical thinking or only one right way of doing or of expressing urgency.

Consider if the situation requires action

As examples of white-centeredness are identified, students should ask what harm is being done by centering whiteness in that example. Students should consider if the policy is valuing some young people above others, giving access and power to some above others, rendering some students invisible, or forcing young people to change parts of who they are. In the above policy example, students might say that the policy causes harm because it does not allow for divergent thinking and does not give grace to students who need additional time or thought partnership. Students might say it values urgency over thoughtfulness and will end up rewarding or punishing the same students over and over again. In this case, taking action is required to create a more equitable and emancipatory classroom.

Choose what form of action to take

Once students weigh all the factors and decide that the problem is worth addressing, they must decide how to take action. Do the students need to ask for the problem to be reconsidered by the people who created it? Do they need to research or propose alternatives to the problem? Do they need to educate other community members about the problem? Do they need to solicit input or buy-in? Do they need to use social media or other public platforms to call attention to the problem? Do they need to petition decision makers? Do they need to hold a classroom discussion and vote?

Decide whose responsibility it is to act

Once students identify a problematic example of whiteness, they need to determine who is best positioned to take action. They will need to weigh the implications of setting, the identity of themselves versus others, the intent versus impact of the problem, and the consequences if they do or don't act. By weighing these factors, they can determine who is most likely to succeed in interrupting the problem. It will be so important for students to determine who is least likely to face potential consequences for demanding change. It is important in this step to not place all the responsibility on students, particularly if they are Black and brown, and to recognize the imbalanced power dynamics of Black and brown students having to act on issues of whiteness. The below chart can help students with those calculations.

Setting	Identity (of Self and Others)
♦ People affected by the problematic example (role in the classroom, number of people, & relationship to one another) ♦ Structure of setting where the problem exists (classroom, lunchroom, school-wide, community at large, state, country) ♦ Familiarity student have with the space where the problematic example exists (our classroom, a place we visited, a government office)	♦ Race ♦ Age ♦ Gender ♦ Sex ♦ Experiences ♦ Comfort with identity (recognizing where people are in their identity journeys) ♦ Role in the space (student, teacher, guest, principal)
Intent/Impact	Possible Outcomes If We Don't Act
♦ Policy maker's openness to feedback ♦ Policy's impact on others ♦ The effect the policy intended to have ♦ The effect the policy is having (use data to support)	♦ What other chances will we get? ♦ What are the implications if we get this wrong? ♦ What message does this send? ♦ What unspoken norms will acting/not acting establish/reinforce? ♦ What potential consequences can I face for acting?

2. **Act and assess the results**

Once you have worked with students to determine the best course of action for interrupting the problem, they must make sure the solution did in fact address white-centeredness. Are many voices, many ways of being, and many ways of doing now recognized and celebrated? Does the new way of doing value all young people, and do all people have access to it? Are all students seen and heard? Are young people embraced for who they are, their personhood?

This work does not have to be done in isolation and should not be removed from content development. Every time you introduce a new rubric, a new text, or a new project to young people, use the time you normally use to review expectations to also scrutinize those expectations. This type of thinking, once developed and practiced, should become a regular piece of the learning environment. Students who encouraged toward activism—through inquiry and praxis—will learn to do this work as a natural part of their learning process.

Notes

1. W.E.B. du Bois. ([1903]1995). *The Souls of Black Folk*. New York: Signet Classic, 7.
2. Junot Díaz. (2014). "A Singular Dislocation: An Interview with Junot Díaz and Taryne Jade Taylor." *Paradox,* No. 26, "Sf Now" Edition.
3. David S. Owen. (2007). "Whiteness in du Bois' *The Souls of Black Folk*." *Philosophia Africana*, vol. 10, no. 2: 110.
4. bell hooks. (2015). *Black Looks: Race and Representation*. New York: Routledge, 12.
5. bell hooks. (1997). "Representing Whiteness in the Black Imagination." *Displacing Whiteness,* edited by Ruth Frankenberg. New York: Duke University Press, 339.
6. hooks, 340.
7. Miss Ann—originated in the antebellum era (1815–1861), Becky—originated in the early-to-mid 1990s, and Karen—originated in the 2010s are all forms of an American colloquialism to denote

    women, almost always white, who are entitled, often racist and determined to get what they want. And what they want, to a frequent degree, is the ability to determine where Black and brown bodies may or may not be present.

From Karen Grigsy Bates. (2020). "What's in a 'Karen'?" Retrieved from: https://www.npr.org/2020/07/14/891177904/whats-in-a-karen

8. Peggy McIntosh. (2003). "White Privilege: Unpacking the Invisible Knapsack." *Understanding Prejudice and Discrimination*, edited by Scott Plous. New York: McGraw-Hill, 191–196.

8

Ain't I A Human? Talk About Personhood, Not Production

Protest-in-Context

The 1996 film *Jerry Maguire* popularized one of the most quoted lines in cinematic history. In a telephone shouting brawl, Tom Cruise's character, sports agent Jerry Maguire, struggles to keep Cuba Gooding Jr.'s character, football star Rod Tidwell, as a client, when Tidwell introduces Maguire to what he calls "a family motto." Against the backdrop of Los Angeles-based hip-hop artist L.V.'s song 'The Wrong Come Up,' Tidwell vigorously yelps, "Show me the money!"

While those four can more colloquially denote someone wanting to know how much they'll be paid, they can also signify a demand for *evidence that something has value and is worth an investment of time, energy, and effort.* In effect, "show me the money" underscores that, as a result of a pervasive capitalist construction that defines value through the rigid linearity of tangible economic gain, we have been socialized to see our bodies—and, therefore, the bodies of others, particularly Black and brown

DOI: 10.4324/9781003183365-8

ones—as means of economic production. From data-driven compensation enticing educators to drill-and-kill to incentivizing grades and behavior, this "show me the money" ethic has flattened the roundness of our possibilities and silenced the productive noise of our imagination. We see, across social institutions ranging from schools to nonprofits and from houses of worship to community clinics, the very fabric of human existence being measured by our contribution to the economy. This poses the question: what would it mean to cultivate and experience our classrooms as sites of personhood and not as sites of production? What would it mean to cultivate a classroom of beings rather than a classroom of doings? What would it mean to do pedagogy with a sentiment of "show me your humanity" instead of "show me the money"?

Talking about personhood, not production should not be confused with the countless writings in the marketplace on asset-based pedagogy, which focuses on the strengths [of thought, speech, and production] that students bring to the classroom, and remains a direct response to deficit-based models of pedagogy, which by their name, focus on the perceived deficits and/or weaknesses of students. *Personhood-pedagogy* emerges out of a sense of radical humanization whereby classrooms create the conditions for students *to be* in a way that embodies the full, complex, shambolic, and evolving essence of their humanity. In fact, personhood-pedagogy supersedes any kind of demand for production as a basis for value and worth. As a counter to the racist, classist, and ableist industrialized systems of knowledge-manufacturing and assessment-marginalization that reify structural barriers against Black, brown, and economically vulnerable students, personhood-pedagogy is about privileging the inherent and basal nature of being human, which provides each student with the right [and rite] to "to be conscious of and make decisions about her uniquely embodied existence in the world."[1] At the heart of personhood-pedagogy is a nuanced but necessary embrace of *freedom* in classrooms. Simone de Beauvoir, the French writer, public intellectual, and existentialist philosopher wrote:

> Freedom is the source from which all significations and all values spring. It is the original condition of all justification of existence. The [one] who seeks to justify [their] life must want freedom itself absolutely and above everything else ... To will oneself moral and to will oneself free are one and the same decision.[2]

Freedom, itself, is not nuanced, but our individual understandings and renderings of freedom within the human existence, particularly relative to young people, certainly are. For many educators, there are limitations to the extent of which young people, namely students in classrooms, should be free. Yet, educators committed to pedagogical parrhesia must undertake the work of deconstructing our subjectivities about student freedom in the ways that we would demand others to deconstruct their subjectivities about *our* freedom. Personhood pedagogy is grounded in and builds upon the inherent value of human existence as an end unto itself. It recognizes that freedom is a student's innate choice to think, speak, and act on life in ways that are most authentic to themselves without any imposition put upon them by us, as educators, to perform or produce in ways that are manufactured, utilitarian, or economic. Therein lies the paradoxical reality of classrooms as sites of knowledge: the perceived [cultural, political, and economic] value of educators is based on their capacity to mercilessly push students into productivity for a nation whose pledge to its flag calls for, "*liberty* and justice for all." For so many, the classroom, then, is a site that embodies a fundamental contradiction: educators [who believe in freedom as a duty] restricting the freedom of students [who believe in freedom as a duty]. From this view, both the educator and the student are production cogs within an industrialized system of teaching and learning, each looking to the other for freedom *to be*. Therefore, personhood-pedagogy asks us to cultivate classrooms as sites for students [and educators] to pursue full humanity, and consequently, as sites of resistance and *duty* against any tactics, mechanisms, pedagogies, or assessments that perpetuate industrialization over being.

On May 29, 1851, at the Ohio Women's Rights Convention, an account was recorded by Frances Gage that a formerly enslaved woman, given the name Isabella Baumfree at birth but better known as Sojourner Truth, spoke to extemporaneously demand her right to full humanity, her personhood as a Black woman in America. While the exact wording of her speech has been contested, the refrain we have become familiar with, "Ain't I a Woman?," reverberates as a call for to privilege *being* as sufficient grounds for freedom, justice, and equity. While Sojourner Truth's refrain, and her speech overall, must be understood, as bell hooks explored at length, as an avowal of the singular struggles that Black women in America survive, we can imagine, in its echoes that so many of our Black, brown, and economically vulnerable students are deliberating from their seats in our classrooms, "Ain't I a Human?" By depriving students of their individual liberation and limiting the boundaries of their identities-being and identities-making, our classrooms render young people as *things, entities, and objects,* effectively rendering the classroom as a site of dehumanization.

To create community within personhood-pedagogy, however, is to place our hope in the constructive possibilities of abolition. Abolition, defined in this sense, is a passionately human, but no less divine, way of defying and deconstructing any systems of dehumanization and oppression that impede the freedom of personhood [most urgently for marginalized folx]. Sojourner Truth, as an abolitionist, envisioned a passionately human way of being that defied a need to declare personhood. We, too, must envision our classrooms as abolitionist spaces, thereby detaching the self-awareness, self-dignity, and self-evolution of students from what they are able to produce, create, or show in the classroom. To do so, we must free ourselves from the imposition of "standardizing," which has become a form of colonialization to the extent that notions like "creativity" and "independence" and "originality" and "authenticity" are merely jargons of the industrialized empire that work to suppress personhood. Standardization in public schools and industrialization in the labor economy have gone hand in hand since the origin of "factory schools" in nineteenth century Prussia, a model replicated in the United States during the early years of the Industrial Revolution.

> Workers who had always spent their working days in a domestic setting, had to be taught to follow orders, to respect the space and property rights of others, be punctual, docile, and sober. The early industrial capitalists spent a great deal of effort and time in the social conditioning of their labor force, especially in Sunday schools which were designed to inculcate middle class values and attitudes, so as to make the workers more susceptible to the incentives that the factory needed and to "train the lower classes in the habits of industry and piety."[3]

What we have now, in many classrooms today is pedagogy—while oft shrouded in asset-based language—as a technologically savvy reincarnation of teaching as the social conditioning of our labor force. As resistance, then, personhood pedagogy is an antidote to the choreography of production that threatens to co-opt the minds, bodies, and spirits of students. What, then, would it look like in classrooms across the nation, namely in classrooms full of Black and Brown students, economically vulnerable and queer students to measure the task and consequence of pedagogy as one's personhood and one's liberation from systems, practices, protocols, policies, and oppressions that limit the embodiment of freedom? What would a student being, identity-liberating, or freedom-seeking protocol look like versus a student work protocol? In so many of our classrooms, we often relate terms like "freedom" and "justice" and "equity" in relation to political ideas like the Constitution, legislative bills, and Supreme Court decisions, but seldom do we relate those same terms to our inherent being. Rarely do we treat every day at the threshold of classrooms and the do-nows of instruction as opportunities for students to encounter the significance and meaning of their freedom as a matter of simply being.

Consequently, our accentuation on *doing* has seeped into our hallways, classrooms, cafeterias, gymnasiums, and even our playgrounds. Within the context of a standards-centered, data-driven, assessments-entrancing, show-your-work-for-full-credit educational complex, we are inclined to presume that creating a context where students detach being from doing is more costly than it sounds. Except, it's not (*it's really not!*). Teaching students to detach from the incessant need to prove the worth of their being is costly; and teaching students to detach their understanding and attainment of freedom from economic productivity is costly. But failing to teach students how to make and live out declarations of freedom—as passionately human, but no less divine protesters—is costlier.

As teachers of protest, *pedagogical parrhesiastics*, we can only cultivate our classrooms as sites of personhood over production by freeing ourselves first. This is no simplistic notion. I am aiming to elucidate the possibilities that speak to, first and foremost, individual freedom—a reclaiming and rediscovering of one's own personhood transcendent of one's productive value within a teaching and learning community. This inwardly concentrated, self-centric liberation is essential to a communal consciousness through which an educator can proceed with a lived, liberatory knowledge of the freedoms and selfhood that their students are pursuing. Freed educators who have moved beyond the futility and despair of seeing themselves as powerless within the classroom now embody the parrhesiastic value of hope. In return, they create a canvas of hope on which the entire classroom, school, and community can do the work of envisioning a freer and more just future in which all oppressed humanity is invited *to be*. When we cultivate a classroom culture, utilize pedagogical methods, and contextualize our teaching and learning communities in ways that reify what it means to be freed humans, we create the conditions for personhood to be a consciousness, a state of mind, and a being.

The significance and complexity of personhood pedagogy as a critical educational process cannot be overstated here. It is what Paulo Freire calls "problem posing,"[4] whereby educators and students engage in critical and generative dialogue to experience an increased consciousness of one's *being* in the world, and whereby consciousness of *being* should provoke "ongoing questions that often challenge old assumptions [and biases and prejudices and predispositions] and [create] the consideration of new possibilities."[5] In pursuit of personhood over production as the lens by which we do pedagogy, accessing a living and embodied freedom for young folx is disassociated from doing and producing and creating and assessing and grading and completing. Instead, freedom becomes linked to a pursuit of the vastness of one's self, fully existent, steadily becoming, abundantly affirmed, and transformatively truthful with one's personhood in the world. In pedagogical parrhesia, protest classrooms are not about producing *things* on the basis of value for the capitalist project of empire, but rather are about being *human* as a moral demand for freedom, a plea to be fully one's self.

Protest-in-Practice

In my early years of teaching, I taught a young girl named Melanie; she was high-energy, athletic, and always ready to make you laugh. She was born under complicated circumstances that left her with significant learning and some physical divergence. At the age of eight, she struggled with fine motor skills, letter/sound associations, and basic number sense—all productive elements of the classroom. That entire year, I taught my lessons to the class and then sat with her and retaught the same objective at a slower pace and with more visuals. My principal and I celebrated when she somehow received a less-than-terrible grade on the state exams, and we happily sent her along to fourth grade without any additional tools to support her in her learning journey. Four years later, when she came back from her middle school to visit me, she walked in and asked, "How is your sister? Still stealing her clothes? How about Creon and DJ? They still fight all the time?" Melanie, a girl who struggled to retain even the most foundational academic content, recalled an inane story I had told about a high school-aged fight I had with my sister and remembered my two cats, who I rarely talked about. Looking back, I recognize how I had failed to understand Melanie as a person and to appreciate her inherent value for stories, her eagerness for relationships, and her memories of the smallest details in the lives of those she cared about.

If I had taken the time to understand her personhood as core to our pedagogical pursuits, to ask her questions about when she felt most seen, heard, and valued as a human, then I would have been able to support her in discovering her strengths as a learner. Further, I *may* have been able to support her in finding and naming ways to leverage those strengths in learning, internalizing, and making meaning of new content. If I had been attuned to the presence of storytelling in her being, I may have been able to facilitate her learning through oral pedagogical strategies knowledge demonstration more authentic to who she was as a human, instead of asking her to display knowledge as a producer through a mass industrialization approach. It is of utmost importance for teachers to get to know their students, not by passing out surveys and playing people bingo but, instead, by building relationships through moments of authentic conversation—conversations that provide opportunities for frank, dangerous, critical, and hopeful conversations that invite lived knowledge of personhood.

Before class begins, after class ends, transitioning to new periods, through fast emails and video chats, in Zoom breakout rooms and Blackboard discussion journals, teachers can have small but meaningful interactions with individual or small groups of students.

1. **Find ways to connect:** share as much as you receive. Don't expect students to share parts of themselves if you are not willing to do the same.

    a. Do you and your student(s) have music, shows, foods, sports, celebrities, art, or hobbies in common or do you have strong opposing views?
    b. Do you have similar family structures or family structures that are completely different?
    c. Do you and your students have similar pet peeves, or do you do things that are pet peeves to some of your students?
    d. Do your students have knowledge, experiences, or interests that are new and exciting to you? That you want to know more about?

2. **Find areas to debate:** once you find common ground or areas of interest for the young people, engage in a nuanced conversation about the topic(s). Sharing differing opinions or alternatives gives perspective but also creates organic conversation. This can be especially exciting when you know nothing about a topic and you rely on your students to teach you. For example, if students have a particular passion for a specific narrative series—YA novels, comic books, anime, streaming video, or beyond—you can debate the best storylines, characters, relationships, story arcs, and so on. Even if you know nothing about the topic, you can ask students to educate you and explore the topic on your own.

3. **Tap back:** Do not fall into the trap of making what you know about the students a gimmick. Nor will you have to time to always return to in-depth discussion on these

topics. Instead, come back to the topic(s) when they naturally fit into conversations or can be used to better explore instructional content.

Once, while facilitating a small white affinity space for aspiring educators, a young man in the group confessed that he was feeling worried that he might not connect with his students, most of whom would be Black and Latinx. "I'm from a strong Italian family. What if their home structures and life experiences are just so different from mine that I don't know how to give them advice and support?"

I asked him if all his friends were white Italian men from Queens who lived with their parents and grandparents and wanted to become teachers.

"Well, no, but those are my friends," he told me. "Most of us grew up together. We share stories, experiences and our own culture. But as a teacher, I worry I won't be able to give direction and help them with issues if I cannot connect."

"Is that your job?" I asked. "Is it your job to have all of the answers? Is it your job to *give* direction and help *them* with issues?"

He looked confused. "Well, I'm their teacher. It's my job to understand their lives and give them advice." The other two participants in the group nodded their agreement.

This was the moment in the conversation when I realized that these aspiring teachers were so worried about being experts that they risked falling into the same traps that I did with Melanie. I asked the three of them to tell me what they thought their job was as a teacher and what they thought their roles were in their students' lives. We needed to spend time redefining not only their perceived roles as teachers but the personhood of their students outside of their roles as teachers. I needed to help them reimagine their roles as *holders of knowledge* to *facilitators of knowledge*. From producers to persons. To do this, teachers need to ask themselves:

1. Can I ask the student to teach me something instead of assuming I know or don't know everything?
2. Can I elicit thinking instead of asking for a complete thought?
3. Can I ask a question instead of making a statement?
4. Can I tell a story instead of give advice?

Meta-Identity Approach

Theories about learning often invoke *metacognition,* the act of thinking about our thinking in order to arrive at insights about our learning—how we do it, why we do it in a specific way, and what that way of learning tells us about how we absorb and internalize knowledge. Yet, in pedagogical parrhesia, we must introduce our classrooms to a personhood framework, a *meta-identity* approach that begin with a "who" question instead of a "what" question. The prefix "meta-" adds the layers of "at a higher order of development" and/or "more comprehensive" and/or "more expansive," so this who-based meta-identity approach refers to active, higher-order processing through reflecting on, monitoring, self-discovering, evolving, and directing the personhood process. When students probe the depths of their personhood, they do more than deepen their learning. They also begin to ask and answer human questions: Who am I when I am happiest in life? How do I become the type of human that is most authentic in the world? What are the conditions that yield the clearest state of my identity?

Five Strategies to Improve Meta-Identity

1. **Provide students with opportunities to reflect on their identities**
   In both academic and non-academic contexts, who students are affects how they learn. Beyond asking students to report on their moods daily, we should give students the chance to share how their identities impact their

learning. To begin, students should create identities maps and then regularly return to those maps when reflecting on learning. To begin identities-mapping, I strongly recommend exploring the classroom resources on identities that are provided by *Learning for Justice*.[6] Once students understand what personal identity is, one exercise that I have done to orient students to one another as they reflect on identities is called, "You Bring/I Bring." In this exercise:

a. Ask students to make a list of ten things that are true about their identity. Help them consider factors like sex, race, ethnicity, religion, gender, physical attributes, family structure, learning style, physical ability, language, neighborhood, and culture.
b. Put students into partnerships. Have them look directly at one another and take turns saying what they bring into the class.
c. At the start of each turn, the person echoes what they heard ("you bring ____") and then adds what they bring ("I bring ____") For example, I might say: "I bring being a woman." Then my partner would say: "You bring being a woman. I bring ____."
d. Once each partner has shared all of their identifiers, bring the class back together to share one identifier they bring that they did not hear their partner say.

2. **Demonstrate meta-identity modeling courageously**

You can do this by thinking out loud, not only about learning content, but also about how the content is affecting you. For example, during a read-aloud, you might return to your own identities map and say:

As a little sister, myself, I am getting really frustrated watching how this girl is being treated by her older siblings. I don't like it when my sisters don't take me seriously, so it is hard for me to read this and see it happening to her.

Or, when you are reading about a moment in history, relate it to your own identities without *centering* your identities, particularly if you are a white educator in predominantly Black and brown teaching spaces. For example:

As a White woman, I am feeling conflicted as we read about the Seneca Falls Convention. I want to be proud of this moment in time and how it laid the groundwork for the freedoms I enjoy today, like having the right to vote, but I also recognize that so many people who did not look like me were denied a seat at the table.

Even as you teach and solve math problems, you can model this type of identity work:

I have to admit that doing these percentages gives me some anxiety, because, when I don't get to use a calculator, I know I struggle to solve problems in my head and sometimes don't trust my mental math, but here's how I am going to work through that fear...

3. **Invite students to keep identity and personhood journals**

In the same way that you model how your identities impact your learning, have students use their identities maps to reflect on their own learning experiences. At the end of a lesson, you might prompt your students to pull out their identities maps and consider one aspect their identities that affected their learning. For example, you might prompt:

Looking at your identities maps, which of your identities were most present for you today as we were learning about ____ and how did those help or get in the way of your learning?

I can imagine, returning to the example of the Seneca Falls Convention, that students might talk about the pride, shame, or confusion that surfaced in them as they considered their own race or gender or sexuality—given how often curriculum talks about "wives" and "husbands" when analyzing the Convention—in relation to the content. This is not, to be clear, asking students to role-play, imagine themselves in another time, or asking them to take on the identities of another person. If you feel that inclination, stop immediately! Students are simply connecting how the learning content relates to who they are. You can also encourage students to do this sort of journaling exercise to reflect on interactions that they had throughout the day and consider how their identities shaped the way they approached or were perceived in a given moment. For example, if students come to class frustrated by an experience at lunch, recommend that they take time to journal about which of their identities most shaped how they showed up and how they were perceived during the interaction.

4. **Utilize a generative dialogue approach to learning**

    I am not a big believer in teacher generated talk-stems to facilitate conversation. These stems can stifle culture and force young people into inauthentic speech patterns that require them to conform to white standards of speech. However, students must be guided to engage in dialogue to practice their listening and *seeing* skills. When learning new content, students must be given space to discuss how identities are showing up in learning. This can be done through thoughtful questioning that orients students to one another's thinking. For example, when reading a new text or studying historical perspectives, teachers and students must ask:

    a. What identities are at play and how are they shaping what I am learning?
    b. When I hear ____ (fellow student's) reaction, how do I think their identities are shaping what they are saying?

c. Which of my identities is shaping the way I am processing this information? How? Why?
   d. How might our identities shape our shared or differing perspectives?
   e. Is my perspective disregarding or undervaluing someone else's identity?

5. **Assign "Am Now" collaborative tasks**

   Unlike the conventional "Do Now," which are individual performative tasks either demonstrating knowledge as a review or assessing foundational knowledge for the day's new content, the "Am Now" is a communal moment to explore personhood. As students enter the classroom, give them a bag or box of two personhood questions and a number. The numbers pair the students with each other. As the partners move to their desks/area of the classroom, they have seven-to-ten minutes to answer the "Am Now" questions. By communally engaging identity questions—of course, ensuring that the questions are relevant to their developmental stages and ages—not only will students be thinking about *their* personhood, but they will also be thinking about personhood in the peers and more universally. Examples of questions include:

   a. Who am I in relation to what I am learning? Do I *see* myself in what I'm learning? (Explain that one can see oneself literally, as in representation, and one can see oneself metaphorically, as in connecting with the content emotionally.)
   b. How is who I am shaped by what happened in the past?
   c. What I am learning now that might differ from how I've been shaped in the past?
   d. What about who I am is influencing how I am processing this content?

e. How does what I am learning affect how my identity is perceived today?
   f. Are there aspects of my identity that might makes others or myself assume I will not be successful in this learning? Why? How does that make me feel?
   g. How am I feeling about what I am learning in relation to my identity?

Notes

1. Sheryl J. Lieb, Ph.D. (2015). *In Pursuit of a Pedagogy of Personhood: Existentialism and Possibilities for Educator Liberation.* Dissertation. The University of North Carolina at Greensboro, Greensboro, North Carolina, 89.
2. Simone de Beauvoir. (1976). *The Ethics of Ambiguity.* New York: Kensington Publishing, 24.
3. Joel Mokyr. (2001). "The Rise and Fall of the Factory System: Technology, Firms, and Households since the Industrial Revolution." Present Paper. Carnegie-Rochester Conference on Macroeconomics, 10.
4. Paul Freire. (2000). *Pedagogy of the Oppressed, 30th Anniversary Edition.* New York: Bloomsbury, 84.
5. Lieb, 107.
6. Learning for Justice Lessons. (2020). Retrieved from: https://www.learningforjustice.org/classroom-resources/lessons?keyword=&field_social_justice_domain[39]=39

9

And Ways to Grow: Talk About a Literacy as a Tool

Protest-in-Context

And this is how it began—reading and rainbows.

I recall the spirit and heartiness, the mystery and intrigue of LeVar Burton, host of *Reading Rainbow*, the half-hour educational series that premiered on PBS on July 11, 1983, with one core intent: encouraging young people to read.[1] The show's theme is an indelible part of the experience, and you can listen to it on YouTube by using a smartphone to scan the accompanying QR code.

DOI: 10.4324/9781003183365-9

For thirty minutes, toddler and adolescent imaginations were invited to transcend the mundane boundaries of everyday life. For thirty minutes, children from disinvested communities were enraptured into places far beyond the streets and neighborhoods they called home. For thirty minutes, reading was more than the foundation of knowledge, as it is orthodoxly framed. It was an interlude of cognitive liberation, and thus, planted seedlings of moral consciousness. If freedom, as a notion, a consciousness, an attainment, a right [and rite] is attainable—and this presumes that it is especially after being restricted from so many—then its attainment is made possible through reading and writing. That is, reading and writing are not only foundational skills but tools of protest in the process by which we pursue freedom.

For that Black boy-child, *me,* who sat at the kitchen counter with his eyes fixed on the television in the corner, by the window, between the sink the stove, there was something parrhesiastic about the melodic invitation to go and grow. As an ethic of hope, reading "was also an openness to worlds, an enchantment with possibility, a desire for connection to all that was and was not tangible."[2] Growing up in a family that spanned the ecosystem of education's attainment, reading functioned as the highest and noblest access to knowledge and meaning-making in the world. As a provocation to grow, it was reading that introduced me to the complexity of caring for each other as a method for being human; it was reading that showed me, in a world abounding with racism, sexism, homophobia, and classism, that our pursuit of freedom is replete with testaments of those who repudiated the thought of being restrained on the basis of their identities. But it was also reading that demonstrated that being human, *fully* human, is brimming with pain and disappointment, grief and regret, that can compel you to retreat from community in the name of self-preservation. It was reading that illuminated the dissonance between the rainbows we often conceive of as we contemplate our futures—freedom, possibility, and hope—and the shadowy wastelands that so commonly engulf our rainbowy imaginations—injustice, oppression, and subjugation. Turns out that in many ways, reading has a way of telling the story of the disorientation of what it means to be human, while in tandem acquainting us with and immersing us in the parrhesiastic possibilities of defying and deconstructing any and all of the systems that bind us from the fullness of our personhood. In the practice of becoming human, and in the pursuit of freedom, for Black and brown folx, queer folx and economically vulnerable folx, reading becomes a kind of sacred performance of imaginative discoveries about ourselves as much as generative learnings about the world in which we are pursuing freedom.

And that is how our growth begins. Reading.

For so many of us in our earliest years of life, before our words were sensible and our sentences were functional, we were inculcated with messages of the limitless dominance of reading and writing. Phrases like, "readers are leaders," "take a look, read a book," and "read, lead, succeed," were meant to instill a longing for literacy within us. In Black and brown households, from those in which financial capital was restricted to those in which money was plentiful, reading and writing—literacy—functioned as a form of social capital that lessened, though certainly did not eliminate, racial vulnerability and social exploitation. This link between literacy—in Black communities—and the pedagogy we're experiencing in today's classrooms and educational climate is as old as chattel slavery itself in the United States.

In the antebellum South, enslaved Black folx who read and wrote were perceived as intrinsically dangerous to the point that reading and writing were increasingly defined and legislated as seditious skills. There were two uprisings, in particular, which enthused white slaveholders to restrict Black access to reading and writing: the Stono Rebellion of 1739 and the rebellion led by Nat Turner in 1831. Together, these rebellions claimed the lives of more than 75 white folx and more than 100 enslaved Black folx; and each rebellion resulted in new anti-literacy slave codes with escalating punishments for Black folx who attempted learning how to read and write. White slaveholders knew then what we know now: reading and writing, when wielded parrhesiastically are demonstrative tools of protest. Reading, as both a way to discover knowledge and an invitation to make meaning of that knowledge in the world is political. Writing, as a way to accept that invitation by using and creating and redefining words, organizing those words into prose and poetry, and then sharing those words with others is political. This is not a new idea. This is not a new risk.

South Carolina Slave Act, 1740

Whereas, the having slaves taught to write, or suffering them to be employed in writing, may be attended with great inconveniences; Be it enacted, that all and every person and persons whatsoever, who shall hereafter teach or cause any slave or slaves to be taught to write, or shall use or employ any slave as a scribe, in any manner of writing whatsoever, hereafter taught to write, every such person or persons shall, for every such offense, forfeit the sum of one hundred pounds, current money.

Virginia Revised Code, 1819

That all meetings or assemblages of slaves, or free negroes or mulattoes mixing and associating with such slaves at any meeting-house or houses, &c., in the night; or at any SCHOOL OR SCHOOLS for teaching them READING OR WRITING, either in the day or night, under whatsoever pretext, shall be deemed and considered an UNLAWFUL ASSEMBLY; and any justice of a county, &c., wherein such assemblage shall be, either from his own knowledge or the information of others, of such unlawful assemblage, &c., may issue his warrant, directed to any sworn officer or officers, authorizing him or them to enter the house or houses where such unlawful assemblages, &c.,

may be, for the purpose of apprehending or dispersing such slaves, and to inflict corporal punishment on the offender or offenders, at the discretion of any justice of the peace, not exceeding twenty lashes.

Alabama Slave Code, 1833

[S31] Any person who shall attempt to teach any free person of color, or
   slave, to spell, read or write, shall upon conviction thereof by indictment, be fined in a sum of not less than two hundred fifty dollars, nor more than five hundred dollars.

And the unwritten, unspoken, yet understood educational code of 2021 includes: Any Black or brown child who fails to read or write at the point of entering third grade shall, upon compounding oppressive systems of racial dominance, economical vulnerability, housing and food apartheid, and health inequity thereof by generational trauma, be fined by illiteracy with disproportionately higher rates of imprisonment and death.

Reading and writing were politicized in 1740, 1819, and 1833, as they are now, as radically human(e) and racially conscious tools of protest, a lived and breathed protest that offers one the unbounded hope of freedom *to be*, of personhood. Despite the dangers, seen and unseen, thousands of enslaved Black folx shouldered the risks of reading and writing through pit schools—pits in the grounds far out into wooded areas that escaped the surveillance of field masters—as a discipling act during religious gatherings, and in the thickets under the fog of night. With scant resources but a strong commitment to ensuring that more newly freed Black folx could access the frankness, danger, criticality, duty, and hope offered through literacy, independent schools and colleges constructed upon federal emancipation built communal networks for learning. As such, for Black folx, teaching—only second to medicine—was seen and understood as the paramount pathway for building self-sufficient and freed communities. In effect, it was Black folx accessing reading and writing that built the foundation on which this nation could experience the Civil Rights movement and Black Lives Matter. It was Black folx accessing reading and writing that provided the necessary tools for schools to become sites of social, political, and moral consciousness bridging knowledge from classrooms to communities. It was Black folx accessing reading and writing that built the infrastructure for pedagogical parrhesia and personhood pedagogy. And it is now our responsibility as educators to utilize the way we talk and teach about reading and writing to guide students to recognize their capacities for literacy as tools for individual and community freedom, for individual and communal being.

As educators, we so unthoughtfully limit the value of reading and writing in our classrooms to "learning new things" or "visiting places we've never been." Both of these are valid, both are limited. In a nation that is increasingly polarized in ways that mirror 1619 when enslaved Africans arrived on eastern shores in the United States, reading and writing are ways for students to protest imposed ideas and acts that oppress, antagonize, castigate, and enslave folx in today's America. What might it look like to take young people on a reading and writing journey to construct persuasive letters "for the people" that contest the personality-erasure of uniforms? What might it look like to guide young people to read op-eds and write letters of response to the editors sharing their varying perspectives on what they read? What might it look like for a group of young people to co-author a legislative recommendation to the city council, community board, school committee, or congress arguing for equity and justice in funding, capital improvements, and social-emotional staffing in schools and classrooms? What might it look like for students to do textual analyses of proposed bills up for vote in their state legislature? What might it look like for students to create sentence starters that will function as the beginning of their verbal and written testimonies for the mayor's budget or the city council's appropriation recommendations? When age and physical ability and parental consent and legal risks might preclude young people from marching in the streets and protesting at city halls and going to jail in the name of "good trouble," might reading and writing be their acts of protest?

When we find ourselves face-to-face with a young person rejecting opportunities to read and write on the bases of boredom, disinterest, and frustration—all of which exist in classrooms—we must reimagine and reconstruct and reframe the tools of literacy as one of the oldest, if not the oldest, form of protest, the most ancient praxis of challenging unfair and inequitable structures, and the most tested and proven strength of bending the moral arc of the universe toward freedom and justice.

On an ordinary Tuesday, while walking down the sun-lit stairwell on the way back to my office, I heard a delicate and distinct teacher's voice calling me from floors away.

"Dr. Harvey, I have a question!"

I found a safe spot to wait, since we were in the midst of the final transition of the afternoon. You might imagine how many young people were moving through that stairwell. She finally made her way to me, enthusiastically out of breath and motivated to ask her question.

"I know this is a silly question, but I've really wanted to know something. Why do you spell your name, 'rob'?"

I laughed and asked, "Why wouldn't I?"

She smirked, her eyes actively communicating that she's organizing her response with struggle. "Well, to start, because you're an educator. And names are nouns ... proper nouns, and since they're proper nouns, we are supposed to capitalize the first letter of proper names, especially names. You already know this!"

With a smirk on my face, bell hooks on my mind, and Baldwin in my heart, I responded.

> As an educator, what I know is that English—its history and its rules—are a historical byproduct of the white

folx. Anglo-Saxons to be exact. As an educator, what I know is that the association between proper nouns and capitalization is recommended style for languages that use alphabetic script. As an educator, what I know is that all language is a social construct, most of which has been used to socially exploit and politically dominate Black folx, brown folx, and other migrant folx. As an educator, what I know is I know enough about what it "should" be to imagine what it "could" be. So, as an educator, I choose to ignore the history and rules of language—as a matter of resistance—and reimagine the relationship between letters, words, sentences, capitalization, and linguistic rules because all constructed knowledge should be deconstructed and reconstructed at some point.

She smiled, I smiled, and in her reply to an all-staff email sent not too many days after that, she signed her name.
"cynthia G."
Literacy empowers us. It evolves us. It unfetters us. It grows us.

Protest-in-Practice

Before we can teach our students to use the power of language for protest, they must understand how language has been weaponized as a tool of oppression. The first thing that I ask aspiring educators in my *Foundational Literacy* course is: "What is Literacy?" Each year the responses are similar. Most of the students define literacy as some combination of reading, writing, and communicating. Some also define literacy as knowledge of a specific subject. Rarely, and I do mean rarely, does anyone in the class define literacy as a social construct. If we expect young people to reconstruct language into a tool of protest, we must make sure that we all understand the power of words. Language develops in tandem with social, economic, and political realities and so reflects our attitudes and thinking. Language not only expresses ideas and concepts but shapes our thoughts. Literacy is a social construct and a tool of power.

There is an awesome amount of pressure to get the work right when a teacher takes on the responsibility of educating a group of young people to access, become proficient in, and reimagine this construct. That work begins with knowing the history of literacy in this country. Through the exploration of congressional legislation [at the federal levels], court cases, local and community policies, and well-known academic debates, teachers can trace the roots of access given and denied through this construct. As my students study our linguistic history through education policy and legislation like Plessy v. Ferguson, Brown v. Board of Ed, Washington v. Davis, Milken v. Bradley, the implementation of voucher systems, No Child Left Behind legislation, and the coining of the concept of the achievement gap, to name a few, we ask ourselves the following:

1. Who is being given access and who is being denied access?
2. Who is making the decisions for and about young people?
3. Which young people are being considered?
4. Who was deciding what is and is not considered a high-quality education?
5. Who was or is deciding what "English" is?

The clearer it becomes that literacy education is a tool of power, the more we recognize the need to study the actual construction of language in this country and consider how language itself is used to dehumanize. We explore common color symbolism, political terminology, and commonly used qualifying adjectives, and we research the history of common phrases, idioms, and vocabulary. This unpacking of language is an activity I expect my teaching candidates to do with their own students. I teach them to ask students:

1. That's an interesting expression. Do you know where that comes from?
2. Why did you choose that word or adjective? What image does it bring to mind?

3. Do you know the history of that word?
4. Can you look that expression up and tell me where it comes from?
5. Who are you celebrating or insulting when you choose to use that word or phrase?

I often find myself asking teachers to consider their language choices. When they use common phrases, idioms, or language to define their identities, I frequently ask them to tell me what they know about the words and turns of speech they choose to use. For example, when a white teacher who was mentoring a Black teaching resident told me that she was unsure of how to support her resident with EdTPA because she was "grandfathered in through the old system," I asked her if she was aware of the history of "the grandfather clause." Because she did not know that *"being grandfathered into something"* referred to a law that restricted many Black folks from voting while ensuring voting rights for many white folks, she could not possibly have understood how her language was reinforcing the racist systems our country was built on. In the same way, when I ask teachers to identify racially, I always follow up by asking them how the history of the word they chose represents what they want to tell the world about themselves. "Why," I might ask, "do you choose Hispanic? What in the origins of that word speaks to who you are?" Or "What is the message you are sending when you choose to identify as Caucasian instead of white?" In the same way that I expect my teachers to understand the history of the language they use, I ask that they guide their students to do the same.

One strategy to develop shared language that educators can use is to come to an agreed-upon set of language norms early in the school year that they will use in their classrooms. A good place to start is with language that the classroom of young people will use as part of their learning process:

1. Have students share a story of when they felt seen or valued by an adult; and ask students to consider and reflect on the language that person used to speak to or about them. In the spirit of meta-identity work, think about how the language used either enforced or deconstructed power.
2. Have students share a story, in small groups, of when they felt invisible or less than a whole person; and ask students to consider and reflect on the language that person used to speak to or about them. What about the words—either their formal definitions, colloquial uses, or emotive triggers—catalyzed those feelings of invisibility or diminishment?
3. Generate a list of words either for identity categories, for learning, or for classroom vows and agreements that students prefer or reject. Make sure that students always explain why. For words that are preferred by most students or for words that the class cannot come to consensus on, ask students to research the origins of the word and consider the implications.
4. Create an agreed-upon list of "preferred" and "rejected" words, along with scenarios to have students roleplay using the agreed-upon language. By roleplaying, students will have the opportunity to assess whether or not the "preferred" words are as communally aligned in practice as they are in theory.
5. Have students audit classroom materials (i.e. syllabi, texts, handouts, etc.) to determine if the language meets the agreed upon norms.

Through this careful study and implementation of language, young people can begin to reconstruct the ways in which they allow the world to talk about them and present themselves to the world. In so doing, student can take the first steps toward demanding that they be seen and treated as fully human.

Notes

1. Reading Rainbow theme song (1983–1999), written by Steve Horelick and Dennis Neil Kleinman, and performed by Tina Fabrique. In 2000, this version was replaced by a version by artist Chaka Khan.
2. Ashon Crawley. (2018). "Black. Queer. Born Again." **Aeon**. Online publication. Retrieved from: https://aeon.co/essays/black-queer-born-again-a-life-in-and-out-of-the-church

10

The World Can't Take It Away: Talk About Joy

Protest-in-Context

It was our typical Sunday morning routine. We pulled up to 4424 Washington Boulevard in St. Louis, Missouri, a little before 8:30am. I recall my theatrical torment turned idyllic acceptance, when I was seven or eight years old, when I had to wake to attend Sunday School, a series of classes that preceded our 10:00am worship service and that offered spiritual formation. For a period, I was the Sunday School musician, particularly because I was a Black male child learning to play piano, and the wiser folx of our church—like my grandmother, Alma, and a great cloud of others—believed that extending me the opportunity would add to my confidence. At about 9:30am, each class would dismiss and assemble communally in our basement fellowship hall to sing a hymn and announce the classes that had the largest attendance and raised the highest offering. During the weekend, I would rehearse countless hymns from the *Red Book*, as it was tenderly called, also known as the New National Baptist Hymnal. In reflection, the only reason I rehearsed is because of the unrelenting nudging of my mother, and my piano teacher during that time, Mr. Gibson. As I'd rehearse, plucking away trying to learn new hymns, I already knew what they'd sing. It rarely deviated. *No. 181: 'Pass Me Not,' No. 191: Glory to His Name,' or 'This Joy That I Have.'* That last hymn would continue to resonate years later, particularly as I waded the waters of identities-discovery and depression, pain and possibilities, disappointment and elation. As a type of hymnic resistance, I am still held by its words, which ushers an ancestral reminder of internal agency that transcends the oppressions of the world:

> *This joy that I have,*
>   *the world didn't give it to me.*
> *This joy that I have,*
>   *the world didn't give it to me.*
> *This joy that I have,*
>   *the world didn't give it to me.*
> *The world didn't give it*
>   *and the world can't take it away.*

In a nation defined by a capitalist sensibility of attainment, consumption, occupation, corruption, annexation, deprivation, taxation, appropriation, and depletion, *joy*—in the hymnic sense of being ungiven and, consequently, unable to be taken— offers us a new construct of protest. It is a construct not unlike the antiphonal, or call-and-response, singing of hymns: the *call* of whiteness attempting to dominate every aspect of Black and brown being, and our *response* affirming, "this joy I have, you didn't get it to me, and you can't take it away." Being captured in the capitalistic cycle of anxiety, never knowing what will be stripped from you, joy becomes untrappable. The portion of our being, or the dimension of our personhood, that we assert before and conserve from whiteness's brutal gaze, its appetite to power and privilege, is joy embodied. Joy, not as production limited by its response to whiteness, but joy in the *flesh*.

Hortense Spillers, a literary critic and feminist scholar, distinguishes "body" from "flesh" to better define the oppression that occurs *on* and the power that is wielded *over* Black people. Black bodies. Spillers writes, "I would make a distinction in this case between 'body' and 'flesh' and that distinction as the central one between captive and liberated subject-positions. In that sense, before the 'body' there is 'flesh.'"[1] Here, she is referring to flesh as the socio-political being that tells the stories of the body. Those stories told of the body, by flesh—the marked, unseen parts of our being in relationship to the world—are scientific and spiritual, political and medical, economic and educational, psychological and emotional. Through joy in the flesh, then, we bring ourselves closer to the conditions of liberation.

The work of pedagogical parrhesia as *joy work*—joy borne of hope—is not about guiding students to reclaim themselves from the gaze and hegemony of whiteness, because "reclaiming" assumes that they could be or had been claimed. Instead, pedagogical parrhesia asserts joy as the primary narrative by which students navigate the stories they tell about themselves, their minds, and their bodies. The assertion of joy in the flesh—transcending what is thought and said about the mind and body—in a world intent on claiming the joy of Black and brown folx is the purest act of protest, since it refuses the stories that whiteness has imposed a story on us: deficiency, disadvantage, and deprivation. Thus, when joy is in the flesh, "the world can't take it away," because it is a story marked on our bodies reserved for our own consumption and proclamation. In her 1978 essay on women subverting oppression and cultural misuse, Audre Lorde writes:

> There are many kinds of power, used and unused, acknowledged or otherwise … In order to perpetuate itself, every oppression must corrupt or distort those

various sources of power within the culture of the oppressed that can provide energy for change.[2]

For so many Black and brown folx, particularly young people navigating the compounded traumas of a nation that wrestles between betraying and becoming its espoused ideals, joy in the flesh is our "energy for change" that cannot be corrupted or distorted. Think of the calls for "black joy" made amid the civil unrest, traumatic imagery, and profound sense of loss that have come to define a quotidian type of American experience, brutal and banal alike. Joy, B*lack joy*, makes possible a spatial and worldly expression of change that has historically been stripped from us in exchange for a joy that can only be realized in an afterlife. To resist, our joy—B*lack joy, brown joy*—must be more than otherworldly and ethereal; it must entitle us to a sense of belonging to this earth. Defying the paternal and perfectionist rigidity of whiteness, joy with the energy it provides for change, enfleshes the messiness of what it means to be human in pursuit of freedom.

Tragedy has been the commonplace narratives about people of color, our bodies, in this nation. Through local, national, and social media, legislative appeals on congressional floors, and testimonies before the courts, we consume daily a litany of deficit-based narratives about the minds and bodies of Black, brown, non-white, and migrant young folx. But those tragedy-narratives—the majority of which are the result of violence borne of the American criminal-legal industrial complex—are only part of the narrative of our bodily experience. To only tell the tragedy-narratives is a form of social-emotional violence that presumes a unilateralism about what it means to think and talk about the Black and brown experience. Joy in the flesh, however, becomes the other part of that narrative, an experience that is not limited to a produced moment, delineating our ethics, our strategies, our everydayness, and our ways of resistance. Joy in the flesh allows us to express the stories *we* can tell about ourselves, stories that have yet to be told, and stories that have been told wrong. This is what Ashon Crawley calls, "otherwise."

> The otherwise as word, as concept, is to presume that whatever we have is not all that is possible. Otherwise is the enunciation and concept of irreducible possibility, irreducible capacity, to create change, to be something else, to explore, to imagine, to live fully, freely, vibrantly. Otherwise expresses an unrest and discontent, a seeking to conceive dreams that allow us to wake laughing, tears of joy in our eyes, dreams that have us saying, *I hope this comes true*.[3]

Joy in the flesh, as *otherwise*, is another embodiment of that essential parrhesiastic value discussed earlier, "hope." As hope, in pedagogical parrhesia, sees despair not as an end, but as a means to an end, it is joy that carries us through that despair into that hopeful end and tells our story. Joy is the mechanism—when, in despair as we hope for the otherwise yet to be realized—that moves us from passive acceptance to protest. In that sense, there is a requisite relationship between joy, otherwiseness, and hope, each of which is reliant upon the other for its fullness to be realized. As one of the wisdom-keepers who was part of the village that reared me would say, "They," typically speaking of white folx, "can take everything I got—money, houses, cars, and land—but they can't take my joy, and they can't take my hope. Because they didn't give me my joy, and my hope ain't built on them no way." Now, as a Black male education leader, I find myself attempting to make sense and make meaning of the intersecting traumas plaguing our schools: systemic racism, economic recession, divisive electoral politics, and a rising death toll at the hands of COVID-19 and its variants. And amid that sense-making and meaning-making, embodying joy becomes a form of radical resistance for the sake of self-preservation. Because, without joy, how do I, as a communal leader, keep believing in this nation, generation after generation, as we continue to experience the sociocultural and sociopolitical consequences of racism? How is it possible that I maintain trust that our public education system will one day realize its ideals, so that outcomes are not predictive on the basis of race or zip code?

I recall attending a professional development session in which the facilitator—a white, well-meaning educator of many years, who had recently transitioned from the classroom to follow wellness work—contended, "Making space is the most radical act of decentering one's self in order to center another." While I agreed with him that making space for young people is, in fact, *a* radical act, we diverged in our measurements of whether or not it was "the most" of all radical acts in our classrooms. At first, I wrestled internally with whether or not to speak up and risk the stability of the session, given the room full of well-meaning white folx, many of whom were suffering with what I understood to be guilt—a psycho-emotional desperation to not feel as bad about themselves. But I decided to risk it. The spirit of so many ancestors engulfed me and I recalled thinking to myself, "What the hell—they don't know me. What I have, they can't take, because they can't find it." *Joy*. I raised my hand and waited patiently to be called.

> What if making space, while radical, is not the most radical act of centering one's self in order to center another? What if, in fact, cultivating joy is a more radical act of decentering one's self in order to center another? "Making space" is built on the idea of "making," which means that, as adults, we are responsible for creating something [space] that in turn, allows students to create something [centering themselves]. But what if we decenter ourselves to guide students toward discovering a joy within that extends beyond anything we can create or "make" for students. As custodians of classrooms, not makers of classrooms, is not our burden to shepherd our students

in cultivating a joy that the world can't give them and the world can't take away? If we do that, our students will make their own space—a space where they can center whatever they want to center. Just another way to think about it.

The idea of curating joy within and shepherding Black and brown young folx to curate their own joy through art, music, writing, stillness, and just being one with themselves lights a fire within the deepest parts of my educational soul. Joy in the flesh, as being, ought to compel all of us to conduct a daily self-interrogation and endeavor to pursue it by any means necessary. And when we find ourselves within communities, systems, or structures that attempt to suppress our beings and suppress our votes, lock away our dreams and lock away our children, assess our authenticity and assess our knowledge, we resist their attempts through our joy. As educational custodians charged with caring for children, we must refuse to despair the young souls within our care of joy simply because we don't understand it. If we take joy in the flesh, and its cultivation, seriously, then our responsibility is solely to invite students to reflect on and imagine what their possibilities of joy may look like. So many of our students yearn for joy, but when your life value is defined by the American industrial complex in terms of economic growth, individualistic success, consumption and belongings, and more, it is difficult to come to terms with a transcendent way of being.

Curating joy, as an everyday act in our classrooms, hallways, cafeterias, and offices, stresses the significance of our students embodying a narrative that divests power from the gaze and hegemony of whiteness. To be clear, joy in the flesh, as an ethic of resistance, is not a perfunctory acceptance of freedom unrealized. Not at all! Instead, joy in the flesh, as otherwise, as hope, can see a day when it has the fullness of freedom—a type of freedom that "the world can't take it away."

Protest-in-Practice

Early in my teaching career, there was a lot of talk among newer teachers and teacher preparation programs about using competition, structured movement and noise, reward systems, and managed fun that infused "joy" into the classroom. A teacher, by that logic, would design and curate this manufactured joy as a tool to motivate students during those perfectly timed intervals between urgent instruction. But authentic joy is not formulated or packaged or manufactured or infused to be released at predetermined, lesson-planned times. Joy in the flesh—identified in Protest-in-Context as *real* joy, joy that can't be taken away—is the result of emotional and cognitive safety, humor, accomplishment, comradery, spontaneity, celebration, and love.

For my first few years as a classroom teacher, my young learners and I would start every day by shaking hands at the door, unpacking our materials, completing an academic *Do Now*, and coming together in a class meeting. During those meetings, we would share any fears or concerns we had for the day, give cheers and shoutouts for student accomplishments, review the daily schedule, and set learning goals for ourselves. Sometimes we would play a quick literacy or math game. Rarely (and I do mean rarely!) did we spend time telling stories or sharing human moments. It was not until about halfway through my last year in a fifth-grade classroom, when I was no longer anxious that my students would not learn if I did not set the tone with a firm handshake and a structured *Do Now*, that we started our days differently. That year, my students filtered into the classroom, sometimes dancing to the music playing off the class-compiled playlist ("That's my theme song," someone would inevitably shout). As they arrived, we would chat about our pets, our families, our breakfasts, plans we were excited about, or anxieties we were feeling. I would move around the room with a bundle of bananas, checking in with individual students and making sure that everyone had had a good night's sleep and a healthy breakfast. For the first few minutes, student would either take out work or homework they had not finished from the day before or work on a prompt. The *Do Now* activities were never about academics. I would usually ask students to draw, write, compose, or in some other way design a response to a prompt about their feelings, their friendships, or other aspects of their lives. From the very beginning of the day, I was determined to ensure that students felt comfortable, seen, heard, and cared for. I tried to carry that tone throughout. As an elementary school teacher, I had the luxury of time, but some of the strategies I used can be translated to departmentalized learning spaces as well.

Curating Human Moments. A few years ago, I got a new manager. He started all his team meetings with activities like, "Take ten minutes to send texts, DMs, emails, or make handwritten notes thanking people in your lives for specific things." He would have us share our most embarrassing memories or talk about what color we thought we were and why. He would lead us in meditation or hold space for us to share what was on our minds. At first, I found myself frustrated by these seemingly off-task activities that took up ten of our fifty minutes together, but then I realized how much laughter and conversation these prompts elicited and how many people who had joined the meeting looking drained and tired were actively participating. Since then, I have started every class I teach with *Human Moments*. When I run out of ideas for *Human Moments*, I ask students to plan and facilitate them. This practice is easily translated into K-12 classrooms and can be done daily, weekly, or whenever the class needs a chance to breathe and reset. These moments can set the tone and culture for the class.

Exposing Joy in the World. One day, while teaching a fifth-grade class, Adrian, a chatty, inquisitive, and high-spirited student said, "Why is the news always so sad?" Another student, Elizabeth—never to be called Beth, "because why be a Beth when you be an Elizabeth" as she'd share with classrooms guess—responded: "I'm sure it's not sad *everywhere* in the world. Let's find some *gooooood* news." That's exactly what we did. Every week, at least two days per week, we would intentionally begin our time together taking in some "*gooooood* news" as a way to set a tone of joy as we entered into learning. Eventually, students asked if they could take turns being responsible for exposing joy in the world by sharing stories, newspaper clips, news reels, and YouTube videos with the class that only had to meet one criterion for success: bring joy to the room.

Allowing Off-Task Humor. When I was learning to teach, I remember being told, "Don't smile until Christmas." The idea was that I needed to be serious and set clear expectations before I could let my guard down or I would lose control. But kids crack jokes—usually, let's be honest, at the most inconvenient times. Not smiling when kids are genuinely funny is inauthentic and makes you seem inhuman or impersonal. Last night, for example, as I was trying to explain to my two-year-old daughter the seriousness of not feeding the dog from the table, she passed gas. She looked up at me and with a shocked face said, "Oh no! The table farted." I stopped my lecture to laugh. The day before, I was telling my five-year-old son to clean his room and he started trying to negotiate how much needed to be put away to be considered clean. Frustrated, I asked him why he thought everything was a negotiation, to which he grinned and said, "I'll only admit to always negotiating if you admit that you do it, too." Again, I laughed. In moments like these, we can reprimand, ignore, or laugh at the ridiculousness. When, even in the middle of your math lesson, a young person says something amusing—something that is also not oppressive, dehumanizing, or derogatory about classmates or other humans in the world—don't feel obligated to be scolding. Laugh, take a breath, ask students to regroup, and move toward the learning outcomes. Teachers do not need to always be in control. In fact, what does the need to control humor and laughter say about our ethics of power and privilege? We do not need to fear being pulled off-task or away from a learning target. It is freeing to be human. It is emancipating to laugh.

Allowing Time for Banter. This morning, I listened to my husband spend three minutes bantering with students about which New York City borough could claim the best pizza. This debate had nothing to do with his content, but he jumped into the fray sharing where his own favorite slice came from. When a student who never participates in class turned his camera on to share a passionate opinion, my husband quickly said, "Mike! It's wonderful to see your face. Welcome to the debate." The student laughed and stayed on camera for the rest of the period. Through this banter, he embodied joy in the flesh. He invited participation in a new way, learned more about what motivates the young people, and learned what they look like when they are passionate about a topic. He figured out a little bit more about what engages them in conversation. He also learned that he could use a *pizza-off* for a future classroom celebration.

Bringing in Music. In all cultural traditions, and particularly in cultural traditions borne of the African diaspora, music and dance are a rhythmic vocabulary of freedom and inextricably linked for so many young folx as mediums for expressing the continuum of human emotions. Of those emotions, joy through music and dance is a cathartic form of release. Creating a playlist of community music with your students in community is an emancipatory tool that helps students learn about each other, learn about you, and even learn about the depth and width of musical traditions in the world. Then, taking that playlist to use as students enter the classroom, as transition between periods, as self-guided work music, or as entrance music before presentations can remind students that they are seen, heard, and cared for.

Storytelling. The only thing I that remember about kindergarten was that my teacher had an oversized rabbit who constantly escaped from her cage and wreaked havoc throughout the home. So many of our lessons and classroom meetings began with anecdotes about this rambunctious bunny. It is no surprise, then, that I also remember loving kindergarten. One of the best ways to bring joy into the classroom is to allow young people the space to tell and hear stories. When I first started teaching, I maintained tough boundaries between the students and myself. When students asked me my age, if I had kids, or about my marital status, I would say, "that's not important, let's get back to math." But it is important. Do boundaries matter? Yes. Should those stories be developmentally appropriate? Yes. Do those boundaries have to present us from making any parts of ourselves, our humanity, or our personhood known? No. We spend hours, days, and months, and sometimes years (think about teachers who loop with their students!) together, and students need to know that they can bring their whole selves into the classroom. Students often learn that their whole person is welcomed into a space only when you, the educator, model being whole. By talking about your family, your home, your commute, your successes, and your disasters, you subvert the production ethic of the classroom and allow students to experience radical humanity. Joy, then, happens when you make space for students to know that their voices and the stories they tell matter in community.

Celebrating Accomplishments. Have you ever watched a video of a school having a pep rally for a state test? Adults get up and yell about how hard the young people have worked and students perform classroom chants. This sort of celebration, designed around a systemically racist and whiteness-normed test through which young people are hegemonized to suffer, is not the same as authentically celebrating achievement—defined, in a protest classroom, as the act of following through to completion. If you want to curate joy by commemorating acts of follow-through to completion within and beyond the classroom, then you need to take the time to know what matters to young people. For every student you teach, you should know what they are working to achieve, preserving to follow through, and what their barriers have been. Create a system for students to share their weekly or monthly goals. They can post these goals somewhere in the room and you create ways to check in on their growth toward these goals. Encourage students to ask for support from peers or name when they are having a hard time with a goal. Then, classroom celebrations can be based on growth made, goals met, and fears overcome. For example, if a student shares that they have been babysitting every weekend to save enough money to purchase something meaningful to them and finally makes the needed amount, then that is worth celebrating. If a student has been struggling to get all of their homework in and shows up one day with all of the work done, then that is worth a round of applause. At the core of an emancipating celebration of accomplishments is knowing how *the student* wants to be celebrated.

Celebrating Mistakes. Too often, the production economy, steeped in whiteness, coerces us to neglect the real learning that comes from our mistakes or confusions. One of my favorite classroom activities is "Reframing Disappointment." In this activity, I ask students to share a story of an academic or interpersonal mistake they made. Classmates listen and tell the story back to their peer but highlight what learning opportunities or personal growth they heard. In pedagogy, students can follow the same protocol by sharing a problem or a piece of their work they are struggling with. When students take the time to explain what they did and what is confusing them, it can help them to clarify their thinking. Sometimes, this reveals when students don't actually know where their confusion is grounded. Classmates, then, can ask questions to clarify confusions and/or support each other to work through the struggle. And, in the spirit of emancipating ourselves as we work to emancipate our classrooms, you might find yourself acknowledging a need to teach it differently. Sharing large and small failures welcomes vulnerability and reminds us that, in classrooms of pedagogical protest, hope is the result of growth and understanding, not perfection.

Giving Permission to be Silent. Once a month, when I was a third-grade teacher, we would have a day dedicated to self-guided work. Soft music would play while students read, wrote, completed math or science projects, and occasionally whispered to one another. These were the most peaceful days. No one bickered, no one argued over personal space, and no tears were shed. Students who had completely caught up on work did stretch projects or helped peers while I worked with whichever students were in the need of the most attention. On these days, we had an agreement to limit conversation and noise. Joy in the flesh, against the conditions of a noisy world full of the piercing sounds of inhumanity, sometimes arises from the stillness of silence. As Toni Morrison writes in her novel, *God Help the Child*, "I don't think many people appreciate silence or realize that it is as close to music as you can get."[4]

Notes

1. Hortense Spillers. (1987). "Mama's Baby, Papa's Maybe: An American Grammar Book." *Diacritics*, vol. 17, no. 2: 67.
2. Audre Lorde. (1984). "The Uses of the Erotic." *Sister Outsider*. Berkeley, CA: The Crossing Press, 87–88.
3. Ashon Crawley. (2016). "Otherwise, Ferguson." *Interfictions*, vol. 7. Retrieved from: http://interfictions.com/otherwise-fergusonashon-crawley/
4. Toni Morrison. (2015). *God Help the Child*. New York: Alfred A. Knopf.

Conclusion
On Inconvenience
Robert S. Harvey

Of all the virtues that beguiles the soul of whiteness, convenience is highest of them all. Within the sacramental boundaries of what it means to be American, embody the American way, and worship at the altar of Americanism, convenience is as much a means of being as it is a means of doing. From "what is hidden in the ordinary events of everyday life" to what "is shot through with suffering, death, and destruction",[1] there is an ethic of convenience that has a grip on American consciousness.

"I was in line first."

"Let's just order in, cooking will take too long."

"How much would it cost to get my daughter into Yale?"

"Have we posted our new DEI statement in response to all the murders of Black people?"

"We will secede from *that* school district."

"What if we just suppress the electorate?"

These are just a few of the postures of convenience that endure within every fiber of American praxis. To be clear, this ethic of convenience, particularly as it is enforced on our individual and communal ways of being and doing, is a consequence and conservation of whiteness.

Convenience, then, is the companion of conservatism. Conservatism, as an ideological system, certainly uses notions of convenience in an attempt to maintain a national strata that oppresses the marginalized, but let's go deeper. Convenience as an ethic of Americanism that transcends any single political tradition, is an orientation of human conscience toward the preservation of the present systems of power, temporality, and oppression, and a rejection of calls to change. In this sense it is clear that any compliment of what is expedient and convenient within a socio-political context is inhumane. The appeal of convenience, as a means of being and doing Americanism, is the centrality that it accords whiteness and the secondary status it imposes on all other folx, namely Black and brown folx. In schools and classrooms across the nation, the convenience of scripted curriculum that suggests that "Columbus discovered America" centralizes European whiteness and silences the Indigenous Peoples of the Americas as secondary beings. The convenience of no-excuses discipline and policed aesthetics that suggests a "proper" way centralizes standards of whiteness and erases the fluidity of individual agency.

This ethic of convenience has formed and informed America's societal expectation of the classroom—a site of preservation for the ideals espoused by those who have the most to lose, their power. In his hauntingly pertinent "A Talk to Teachers"—delivered in New York City under the title "The Negro Child-His Self-Image"—James Baldwin illuminates this notion:

> The paradox of education is precisely this—that as one begins to become conscious one begins to examine the society in which he is being educated. The purpose of education, finally, is to create in a person the ability to look at the world for himself, to make his own decisions, to say to himself this is black or this is white, to decide for himself whether there is a God in heaven or not. To ask questions of the universe, and then learn to live with those questions, is the way he achieves his own identity. But no society is really anxious to have that kind of person around. What societies really, ideally, want is a citizenry which will simply obey the rules of society. If a society succeeds in this, that society is about to perish.[2]

To contextualize these words in their particular moment—October 19, 1963—it is critical to realize that that year was defined as one of the most piercingly contentious in the United States at the intersection of race, white supremacy, and political discord. From the assassinations of President John F. Kennedy and NAACP organizer Medgar Evers to the bombing at 16th Street Baptist Church in Birmingham, Alabama, claiming the lives of four little girls, Baldwin was elucidating the burden of the Black experience in America. An experience marked by the countless civil protests in which simply being Black impaled the convenience ethic of whiteness; an experience that mirrors, in many ways, what it means to be Black today. Many of the educators who listened to Baldwin's voice that day, were white, mostly serving the segregated schools and communities still commonplace, despite the Supreme Court's 1954 Brown v. Board of Education decision which ruled, "in the field of public education the doctrine of 'separate but equal' has no place." For those white educators, heirs of American convenience, it becomes clear that the aim of Baldwin's talk was to subvert the convenience pedagogy that asphyxiated schools and classrooms of Black and brown children; and that preserved the hegemonic, banking-model transfer of information that maintained a social apparatus of white power and white privilege.[3]

Indeed, this is a convenience built, in part, on myths about the American historical narrative. Baldwin's central critique of schooling in American, as a core institution for the safeguarding of white convenience, is that its erasure of Black identities is essential to maintaining a myth about white history that, in turns, builds a history of the nation and the world. That is to say, whiteness prolongs its social existence and its dominance through a notion of convenience that lies about its truths in the bitter formation of this nation, in how it has treated the minds and bodies of other humans, and in its espousal of a "land of the free." But this ethic of convenience in schools and classrooms did not and does not emerge *ex nihilo*, which demands us to locate and critically engage its emergence in a systemic ether, whiteness. The convenience of the political disregard for the Flint water crisis or the myriad economically privileged communities nationwide attempting to secede from their school districts is not disconnected from conserving whiteness' fancied aesthetic of equality. That, at heart, is the cultural value of convenience: it eradicates having to deal with, or take seriously, the democratic contradictions, which emerge for Black, brown, indigenous, and non-white folx. Contradictions which did not and do not emerge *ex nihilo*, but rather emerge out of and are defined by convenience.

Baldwin writes,

> The obligation of anyone who thinks of himself as responsible is to examine society and try to change it and to fight it—at no matter what risk. This is the only hope society has. This is the only way societies change.

This obligation holds in *pedagogical parrhesia* and its five pillars: frankness, criticism, danger, duty, and hope. Employing this notion as a way to interpret Baldwin's call to educators, that call becomes:

> The obligation of anyone who thinks of him as responsible **[duty]** is to examine society **[frankness and criticism]** and try to change it and to fight it—at no matter what risk **[danger]**. This is the only hope society has. This is the only way societies change **[hope]**.

Pedagogical parrhesia, then, is unambiguously an ethic of inconvenience. As a notion of disruption. It renders the comfort and preservation of our temporal reality as despairing—and thus, renders hopeful only those realities that when scrutinized and experienced by the oppressed, offer material and immaterial freedom. While those who, by their participation with and proximity to whiteness, experience freedom largely through identities-making with a material advantage, those of us who are Black and brown must measure our freedom, not through accessing the material advantages of a white capitalist empire—but through an immaterial audacity to inconvenience the white capitalist empire as duty. Disruption, in this sense, demands reimagining the boundaries and formation and production of freedom. It is an interrogation that not only reimagines, but also reinvents the possibilities that are produced through and that produces freedom. Parrhesiastically, the audacity to inconvenience prompts the emancipation of our classrooms from sites that cultivate "a citizenry which will simply obey the rules of society" to sites that cultivate a citizenry that is unwilling to regenerate another era of societal rules that tyrannize, hegemonize, and terrorize marginalized folx. It is not an individual audacity, but a communal audacity—promoting a transgressive ethic that disrupts the comfortability of any community, school, and classroom that continues as a bastion of convenience. If convenience is the companion of conservatism—the maintenance of guaranteeing what *has been*, then inconvenience is the companion of progress—a disruptive demand that moralizes a politics of possibilities. Not impassive possibilities, but indignant possibilities, borne of inconvenient struggle and disruptive truth-telling.

This disruptive struggle for progress that yields material and immaterial freedom, inescapably a long road of inconvenience, will ultimately and *only* be a story of educators—Black, brown, white, Indigenous, Asian, and all other identities—embodying the frankness, criticism, danger, duty, and hope of pedagogical parrhesia. But it is not hard to understand why there are so many educators, namely white educators and those who are beneficiaries from their participation in whiteness (the latter begs repeating!), who grapple with and consistently neglect these values. Being disruptive, particularly disruptive of one's own power, to realize progress for others is a complex pursuit. Though some educators—quite possibly many educators—contend that the pursuit is a worthy one, the evidence of how few take the pursuit suggests that the worthiness of disruptive and inconvenient progress is more choreographic than corporeal. I fear the ways in which we have titillated the choreography of possibilities, and fear even more that because of the allure of choreography we have acute misunderstandings of who is conspiring alongside us in our inconvenient struggle toward a disrupted freedom. That is perhaps why white folx—and some Black and brown ones too—with marginally peripheral access to power and privilege in the socio-political economy cling to the ethic of convenience and the conservation of the status quo, while performing the choreography of disruption with their bumper stickers, window and yard signs, tee shirts, and social media antics. Because we cannot deny the ways in which the allure of power for white folx, even marginally, drowns the demands for disruptive progress and inconvenience pedagogical politics reimagining the ways in which *all* of us can access a fuller freedom. This drowning is what dispossess innumerable Black and brown students, teachers, and leaders from actualizing *our* imaginative possibilities produced through freedom because freedom, in the ethic of convenience, becomes nothing more than an unending performance of choreographed promises. To be clear, promises are convenient while actualizations are inconvenient.

When entangled in pursuit of freedom—that is, the knowledge that being critical of society and one's place within society plants seeds of danger, risking power, privilege, and positionality, and consequently, silencing hope for a different world—actualizing the disruptive, revolutionary, and radical possibilities produced by a formation of inconvenience counters the fancied aesthetics of whiteness and its appeal to preserve the material freedoms of those in control. Educators who neglect to embody the inconvenient values of pedagogical parrhesia, are akin to those white Christian clergypersons whom the Reverend Dr. Martin Luther King, Jr. addresses in his noted 1963 "Letter from a Birmingham Jail."

You may well ask: "Why direct action? Why sit ins, marches and so forth? Isn't negotiation a better path?" You are quite right in calling for negotiation. Indeed, this is the very purpose of direct action. Nonviolent direct action seeks to create such a crisis and foster such a tension that a community which has constantly refused to negotiate is forced to confront the issue. It seeks so to dramatize the issue that it can no longer be ignored. My citing the creation of tension as part of the work of the nonviolent resister may sound rather shocking. But I must confess that I am not afraid of the word "tension." I have earnestly opposed violent tension, but there is a type of constructive, nonviolent tension which is necessary for growth. Just as Socrates felt that it was necessary to create a tension in the mind so that individuals could rise from the bondage of myths and half truths to the unfettered realm of creative analysis and objective appraisal, so must we see the need for nonviolent gadflies to create the kind of tension in society that will help men rise from the dark depths of prejudice and racism to the majestic heights of understanding and brotherhood. The purpose of our direct action program is to create a situation so crisis packed that it will inevitably open the door to negotiation.

Plenty of educators—more than we probably care to admit—will ask their colleagues, principals, and district leaders: "Why protest teaching? Why frankness and criticism, danger and duty, and so forth? Isn't something less frank, less critical, less dangerous a better path? Isn't it more convenient to leave *that kind of stuff* to families?" Like King, the only negotiation we can stand—in a moment plagued by intensifying racial dissonance in the name of convenience politics, resulting in convenience pedagogy—is one in which we dramatize the inequities and injustices against Black and brown students to the point where those in power are no longer permitted to preserve the present temporality.

For those who want to be abolitionist—*passionately human, but no less divine*—in our pursuit of emancipating classrooms, there are two dimensions of inconvenience as a counter-ethic that we must consider. First, it is not an ethic limited to any singular individual; and second, it rejects respectability and decency as prerequisite. American whiteness tends to define its ethic of convenience through express individualized fragility and deflect communal responsibility when confronted with the inconveniences compelled by protest. The shift from individual to community accountability, however, is not only a moral shift, but also a pedagogical shift demanding that educators shy away from risking inconvenience to any one student, any singular colleagues, or any particular individual within their teaching and learning ecosystem. Pedagogy informed by inconvenience, instead, acknowledges how oppressive, tyrannical, or unbearable any form of convenience is on and within the lives of Black and brown folx.

One might ask, or be tempted to ask: what are the nuances and exceptions to only privileging the community over the individual? In observing and considering the ways that individuals, despite the myth of self-autonomy, shape and are shaped by interactions with the moral makeup of America, philosopher Albert Borgmann underscores why that is the wrong question. In the following passage, Borgmann is responding to Winston Churchill's 1943 insistence that the rebuilding of Parliament, bombed by the Nazis, be a communal endeavor.

> The individual does not shape buildings. We do it together, after disagreements, discussions, compromises, and decisions. The ways we are shaped by what we have built are neither neutral nor forcible, and since have always assumed that public and common structures have to be one or the other, the intermediate force of our building has remained invisible to us, and that has allowed us to ignore the crucial point: We are always and already

engaged in drawing the outlines of a common way of life, and we have to take responsibility for this fact ... We have to be fair when it comes to judging the kind of life that has been the result of our shared building and common desiring.[4]

Schools, as nation-building and democracy-shaping institutions, must be implicated in Borgmann's analysis of how our public spaces shape our democracy. To disassociate schools—public, private, and parochial—from their roles as democratic institutions is to deny one of Baldwin's core assumptions of education. As democracy-shaping sites, the appeal of privileging the individual, per Borgmann's framing, extends an "out" for those folx who refuse the danger of taking responsibility for their complicity with power while in school— not just the building but the social architecture that it determines for Black and brown folx. Privileging convenience for individuals, as a mechanism for circumventing pedagogical parrhesia, yields dim conditions for educators seeking to steward a classroom toward protest, and hope of reconstruction, in a nation entranced by preservation. This protest-hope is borne of the "disagreements, discussions, compromises, and decisions" made every day by educators, the conductors of democracy within their classrooms.

Let's face one thing: "We can disagree and still love each other unless your disagreement is rooted in my oppression and denial of my humanity and right to exist." These words from novelist Robert Jones, Jr., (often erroneously attributed to James Baldwin), represent the unsaid response to white educators who choose to deny the ethics of inconvenience. We can embrace the danger of disagreement while being conscious enough of one's positionality and privilege to avoid rooting those disagreements in the oppression of another's humanity. Inconvenient pedagogy is moral work, democratic work, communal work—it is risky, troublemaking, and rejects the notions of respectability and decency as prerequisite for parrhesia to be undertaken.

Among the most lamentable American rites are the politics of respectability and decency, a false promise of freedom impressed upon us from our youngest ages. While all of us must take responsibility for freeing ourselves from them, we must do so proportionately to our place in the social strata. This is because Black and brown folx have been shaped by respectability and decency politics at the behest of whiteness. In her 1993 book on women's roles in Black social-religious life in the late nineteenth and early twentieth centuries, Harvard professor Evelyn Brooks Higginbotham named this concept, "politics of respectability." In her analysis, this concept is a form of self-presentation, a social strategy historically employed by Black folx, to distance ourselves from and publicly reject the white-defined stereotype aspects of our communities in order to fit the hegemonic norms of American public culture (i.e. whiteness) standards. Responsibility, enacted through conscious behaviors often taught as the values of decency, such as polite manners, self-help, temperance, meekness, and other socially constructed values of decency, was considered "as the cornerstone for racial uplift"[5] and had dual audiences: Black folx who internalized respectability in order to access fair treatment, and white folx who needed to be convinced that Black folx could present themselves as worth of respect. Higginbotham expounds on the impact of respectability in Black classrooms when she writes:

> When early twentieth-century black educators, clubwomen, and leaders from diverse backgrounds referred to the "New Negro," they linked respectability with proof of the race's uplift from the degradation of slavery and from the disparaging images of Sambo and blackface minstrelsy.[6]

Today, many of the methods employed in schools and classrooms, particularly those that educate predominantly Black and brown young people, are anything but respectful or decent, however. When white, well-meaning educators (and some Black and brown ones too) perpetuate the myth of attaining freedom by way of decency, they end up shunning learners' needs to embody their own authenticity, which is so often inherently inconvenient to the perpetuation of whiteness. We can hear this in the overemphasizing of familiar respectability rhetoric—"tuck your shirt in so you look like a scholar," or "pull those pants up so you look professional," or "it's time to clean up with a haircut, don't you think," or one of the worst, "stand straight, arms to the side, eyes in front of you, feet together, and lips sealed."

Makayla is an eighteen-year-old, Black and queer high school graduate who lives in the NYCHA[7] public housing projects. Attending her zoned school, she is preparing to start her first year at a private, historically Black college. She is thoughtful and leaderly, empathetic and communal, and has a particularly complex understanding of respectability:

> Most of the white teachers I have look at me as if I must be incompetent because of my appearance. From my nails having bejeweled designs to the length and color of my hair to way I know how to go in and out of "hood girl" talk and "proper English" based on my mood and who I'm talking to, they don't know what to do with me. They don't know how to place me. And that's really the problem, I can't be placed, and I refuse to be. Don't get me wrong, it's not always easy being this confident, especially when they start with their microinsults, but I just don't know how to perform for anybody, especially them. And do you know what's craziest about it all? Most of them claim to be so "down," talking about how they went to the George Floyd protests and say things like, "say her name." And I was thinking, you can protest and "say her name" but you can't accept my nail designs and hair color and the way I *choose* to talk to *my* friends? What kind of body policing and respectability stuff is that?

To Makayla and to so many other Black and brown young folx, the politics of respectability and whiteness' criteria for what qualifies as decency functions as a specter that attempts to limit their ability to be. In that sense, any way of being that inconveniences the respectability of whiteness and the institutions shaded in the respectability of whiteness are ways of being that an ethic of convenience endeavors to hegemonize through editing. Spirit-editing. Body-editing. Imagination-editing. Name-editing. This hegemonic editing is rooted in white notions of socioeconomic class and privilege, systemic power and policing, all of which are long-utilized tactics of the American empire to reinforce within-group discord and disruption. In effect, by perpetuating the politics of decency, whiteness endorses a type of intra-oppressive dynamic whereby marginalized folx begin holding each other to respectability performances in order to do whiteness' hegemonic, racialized work for it.

Think of the ways throughout teaching and learning communities—primarily in urban metropolitan areas with dense concentrations of schools borne of the education reform movement—in which uniforms and dress codes were weaponized to enforce a dominant narrative against Black and brown families that correlated suit blazers, button-down and polo shirts, belts, and loafers to improved academic performance. From the essence of that narrative, hoodies, like the one worn by Trayvon Martin that purportedly marked his Black body as threatening, have become synonymous in many school contexts with "unscholarly" or as "having the potential to hide things they shouldn't have." Similarly, the archaic, misogynist treatments of women's and young girls' bodies have, in the tentacles of hyper-and-toxic masculinity, caused schools to measure skirt lengths, regulate denim tightness, and calculate the size and number of holes in jeans. Instead of cultivating school communities of radical transparency and humane accountability where students and educators alike honor the space's shared, co-created agreements by seeing each other's dignity, schools deem articles of clothing as "not approved." Despite the performative notions of progress that so many teaching and learning communities—and the educators who populate those communities—espouse, like those who claimed, as Makayla noticed, to "be down" for justice, the cup of respectability is still being gulped, as crumbs of decency are being chewed. To empty the cup and discard the crumbs would be an inconvenience obliging whiteness to radically humanize the way it sees, hears, affirms, and sacrifices space for Black and brown personhood to transcend its politics of being. It is whiteness giving up the subjugating imagination and plantation reincarnation of Black and brown oversight. Respectability, then, is a sacred veil for white convenience to refuse taking on the daunting task of humanizing Black and brown personhood.

What is protest, pedagogical parrhesia, but an inconvenience to what is? What is protest, pedagogical parrhesia, but the daily reimagining, reciting, and reassuring of what can be? What is protest, pedagogical parrhesia, but a moral demand for power and privilege—imprisoned within the irons of whiteness—to sacrifice itself of its positionality over oppressed minds and bodies? And what is protest, pedagogical parrhesia, but a praxis of hope—borne of our frankness and criticism, danger and duty—that can see an emancipated world, material and immaterial, wherein all marginalized folx are freed to emerge in the fullness of their beings? And what is protest, pedagogical parrhesia, but an inconvenience that disrupts the preservation of our temporal now for a passionately human, but no less divine possibility of tomorrow? And what is protest, pedagogical parrhesia, but an embodiment and fleshing as much as it is a demonstration and movement? A being and a becoming. A doing and evolving. A now-is and a to-be. Pedagogical parrhesia, in the inhumane convenience of American whiteness and its smog on classrooms, is a filtering of the air, eradicating the allergens of colonial supremacy, and inviting Black and brown students to breathe. To see their breath as a communal act of inconvenience that speaks life within as it speaks life into the creation of a "new way, a new world—and even a new witness."[8] If inconvenience is the ethic upon which pedagogical parrhesia is built—and there is no way to suggest that it is not—then we must center the ways that Black and brown bodies are the incarnation of it. What, then, does it mean *to be* an inconvenience? It means being the creator and the created, the instrument and the effect of emancipating possibilities: to see what eyes have not seen, to hear what ears have not heard, to feel what has not entered into the heart of this world.[9] We do not know what will become of our inconvenience, but we do know that it will be freer than this.

Notes

1. Ronald F. Thiemann. (2014). *The Humble Sublime: Secularity and the Politics of Belief.* New York: I.B. Tauris & Co Ltd, 38.
2. James Baldwin. (1963). "A Talk to Teachers." *The Saturday Review*, December 21, 1963.
3. Paulo Freire. (2018). *Pedagogy of the Oppressed, 50th Anniversary Edition.* New York: Bloomsbury Publishing, Inc., 71.
4. Albert Borgmann. (2006). *Real American Ethics: Taking Responsibility for Our Country.* Chicago, IL: The University of Chicago Press, 7–8.
5. Evelyn Brooks Higginbotham. (1993). *Righteous Discontent: The Women's Movement in the Black Baptist Church, 1880–1920.* Cambridge, MA: Harvard University Press, 145.
6. Higginbotham, 195.
7. New York City Housing Authority.
8. Robert S. Harvey. (2021). *Abolitionist Leadership in Schools: Undoing Systemic Injustice through Communally Conscious Education.* New York: Routledge, 208.
9. 1 Corinthians 2:9 (NASB).

For Product Safety Concerns and Information please contact our EU representative GPSR@taylorandfrancis.com
Taylor & Francis Verlag GmbH, Kaufingerstraße 24, 80331 München, Germany

www.ingramcontent.com/pod-product-compliance
Lightning Source LLC
Chambersburg PA
CBHW061828300426

44115CB00013B/2294